districts
that
succeed

districts
that
succeed

breaking the correlation
between race, poverty,
and achievement

KARIN CHENOWETH

HARVARD EDUCATION PRESS
CAMBRIDGE, MASSACHUSETTS

Second Printing, 2021

Paperback ISBN 978-1-68253-626-1
Library Edition ISBN 978-1-68253-627-8

Library of Congress Cataloging-in-Publication Data is on file.

Published by Harvard Education Press,
an imprint of the Harvard Education Publishing Group
Harvard Education Press
8 Story Street
Cambridge, MA 02138

Cover Design: Ciano Design

The typefaces in this book are Clarendon, Gotham, and Hoefler Text.

Contents

Introduction

Since beginning work on *It's Being Done*,[1] published in 2007, I have been to dozens of high performing and rapidly improving schools that serve large percentages of students of color and students from low-income families. Over the years I have shared what I think are important lessons about how these "unexpected," highly functional schools operate. But by the time I had completed my last book, *Schools That Succeed*,[2] I began to explore the district role in school success and in school failure. I realized that you can fix schools all you want; if the districts within which they reside are dysfunctional, the schools will not stay fixed.

I came to this realization after seeing highly functional schools serving children of color and children from low-income homes deteriorate when their principals were replaced by new ones who did not continue the systems and culture that had made the schools successful. Watching them fall apart has driven home to me the importance of school principals. But it also points to the fact that schools are not perpetual motion machines. They are affected by district leaders who are responsible for the hiring and placement of principals. I have noticed that when district leaders understand the need for continuity, and when they support the right kind of new school leaders with strong systems, then schools can continue to improve, even if they sometimes dip for a time. But when district leaders don't understand those things, the schools fall apart.

The question then arises: What do successful districts look like? How do the leaders in them think about improvement and school leadership? What do they do differently? That is the subject of this book.

1

Expanding my lens from schools to districts does not in any way negate the importance of schools. Rather, it is a recognition that schools live within complex ecosystems that affect them in any number of ways, from finances to personnel procedures.

In some ways, we are at a crossroads. Many of the big "reforms," driven by big ideas and big philanthropic dollars, have failed or stalled. The resulting disappointment feeds a larger narrative that public schools are hopelessly defective and incapable of improvement. This, in turn, has nourished a determined political attempt to undermine all democratic public institutions as inherently corrupt and unworthy of tax dollars.

This book will demonstrate that there are educational leaders whose knowledge and skill in running districts can be exposed and shared, to use the language of British education researcher Mel Ainscow.[3] They are not perfect leaders running perfect districts. But they have solved some of the problems that other districts around the country face, and the lessons they have learned should be studied for the wisdom they contain.

ACHIEVEMENT, EQUITY, AND DEMOCRACY

The good news contained in this book is that educators out there know how to make public schools better—a lot better. By systematically exposing their expertise, we can learn how to help all schools get better. The question is not whether we *can* but whether we *will.*

But before we even get to that, I feel the need to state something. It is so obvious, and yet sometimes gets lost in all the debates swirling around public schools that it bears saying: We established schools to help kids get smarter.

Kids aren't born knowing a whole lot, and it is the rare family that can teach them everything they need to know. Every society has had ways to impart knowledge and skill to children, but until the modern era few have ever considered it necessary to teach any but a small few more than the basics.

For most of human history, advanced knowledge was reserved for priests and the sons of rulers, who were taught privately or in small academies dedicated to teaching them their history, their culture, and the principles of governing.

With the founding of the United States came the revolutionary notion of ending the rule of inherited aristocracy, and a more democratic idea of education came into being. For ordinary people to be able to weigh in on the important issues of the day they needed to know quite a bit about history, geography, and science. And they needed familiarity with the literature and art that help us make sense of the human condition and provide us with a common set of metaphors and allegories to illuminate our discourse.

Skeptics who believed most children incapable of learning more than the minimum required for survival were countered by those with a more optimistic view of the capacity of humans to learn. Local communities set up schools both to prepare educated citizens who could wield democratic power wisely and to ensure that our nation had the benefit of talent that previous societies had neglected. Instead of laboring on farms and in mills and factories, more children over time learned to read, write, and cipher, unleashing enormous economic, intellectual, and cultural energy. Every expansion of education saw a greater expansion in our economy and world power, from the initial establishment of grammar schools to the expansion of high schools, land-grant colleges, and the passage of the GI Bill. For the first time in human history, vast numbers of ordinary people with no connections to wealth and power had the opportunity to make their way unimpeded by the obstacles of class, in large part because of the nation's commitment to public education.

Except, of course, the United States has never had an unalloyed commitment to democracy—which means it has never been committed to the education of *all* children, most particularly African American children, who were forbidden from learning to read in much of the pre–Civil War South.

The tension between Americans who believe in a democracy where ordinary people have a say in how they are governed and those who don't has played itself out in endless permutations. And public schools have been key battlefields.

The starkest example comes from the Reconstruction period. One of the first things African Americans in the South did when they were free to act politically after the Civil War was to establish public schools for all children. And when the antidemocratic counterrevolution set in after Reconstruction, one of the first things white Southern aristocrats did was to defund those schools. To make their point even clearer, they burned many schools to the ground and murdered teachers and principals. They knew that schools make kids smarter, and that smarter people are in a stronger position to demand equality and wield power; not only were they unwilling to share power with African American people and Native people, but also with poor white people. Well-funded schools threatened white oligarchs' power, so they did away with them and continued to send their own children to private academies or educate them at home with tutors.

Since then we've had many battles between pro- and antidemocracy forces.

One of the key victories for democracy was the passage of the Voting Rights Act of 1965. It enforced the constitutional right of every adult citizen to vote and thus be part of helping shape local, state, and federal policies. That step toward democracy was accompanied by a national commitment to ensuring that all children receive a quality education, no matter who they were or where they lived. The concrete expression of this commitment was the federal Elementary and Secondary Education Act (ESEA) of 1965, the first part of which (Title 1) sent a huge chunk of money to schools with students living in poverty. For the first time in American history, every child would have access to a quality school with sufficient staffing, books, and materials. Finally, the promise of equality and democracy seemed real.

But here we come to one of the paradoxes of modern American education.

The twentieth-century president arguably most committed to democracy inadvertently undermined public education.

This takes a little bit of telling.

President Lyndon B. Johnson, who pushed, pulled, and pressured Congress into passing the Voting Rights Act and the ESEA, as well as other pro-democracy laws such as the Civil Rights Act of 1964, had been a teacher early in his adulthood. He saw firsthand the corrosive effect of segregation, which had consigned the Mexican American children he taught to schools with few books and inadequate facilities. Johnson was determined to ensure that all children, no matter what their background, had good schools.

And he knew children in those schools would rise to the challenge— because he knew schools make kids smarter.

But he also knew it would be helpful to have intellectual support for his position. So he commissioned a report from a social scientist who compiled a vast quantity of information about American schools, their funding, and their outcomes. Johnson had assumed the data would show that poor children and children of color on average had inadequate schools, and that when they had access to adequate schools they learned as much as white middle-class children.

James Coleman did indeed find that on average poor children and African American children had much less access to books, laboratories, teachers, and other markers of adequate schools. But he found something that shocked not only Johnson but the education world as well. When he controlled for funding and staffing and numbers of books and the other things he could quantify, Coleman found that poor children and children of color didn't achieve at the same level, on average, as white middle-class children.[4] Achievement was more highly correlated with children's backgrounds than with the school characteristics he studied. This was not what Johnson had wanted to hear. He had wanted to hear that schools made kids smarter, and Coleman hadn't found that.

Something often missed in discussions of the Coleman report is that Coleman noted that some schools seemed to have more of an effect than others, particularly for African American children. But this was a tentative finding requiring more research and received little notice.

Another thing often missed was that the measures Coleman used were crudely quantitative and didn't capture anything about curriculum or instruction—or what we would call school quality. He was working with the data he had, not all the data required. And the data he had couldn't answer the question *why* achievement was correlated with student background.

Johnson understood how devastating the Coleman report might be to his pro-democracy agenda and tried to bury it by releasing it on the

Friday of the Fourth of July weekend. His subterfuge didn't work. Over the subsequent decades, the Coleman report went on to become one of the most—if not *the* most—influential pieces of social science ever published. It has launched thousands of spin-off studies demonstrating the correlation between poverty, ethnicity, and low academic achievement, and it remains the cornerstone piece of research assigned to future teachers and principals.

The effects have been devastating. Among other things, the Coleman report and its successors have provided a rationale to those who were looking to oppose adequate schooling for all children. It doesn't matter, they say, how good schools are; kids come in with whatever smarts they have—due to nature or nurture or both—and schools can't make them smarter.

Those who believe in democracy have continued to push for better-funded schools, particularly for children of color and children from low-income families. But they are continually faced with the argument that children of color and children born into poverty are already so damaged there is little schools can do to educate them. For a couple of decades at the end of the twentieth century and the beginning of the twenty-first, the argument that African American children are incapable of high achievement became socially unacceptable and was replaced with semi-polite euphemisms about family culture rather than direct language about race. But the racist argument that, on average, African American children are intellectually deficient—the lie told to justify slavery, segregation, and oligarchy—was kept alive in those years by pseudo-intellectuals like Charles Murray.[5] In recent years that lie has roared back, predictably accompanied by the antidemocratic efforts to restrict voting in ways that especially disenfranchise African Americans, immigrants, and people with low incomes. As in the post-Reconstruction period, antidemocratic efforts and the movement to underfund and undermine public schools have gone hand in hand.

Meanwhile, despite notable success stories, public schools have failed at scale to break the correlation that Coleman found between achievement and socioeconomic status.[6]

The social scientist who is probably closest to being Coleman's intellectual heir is Sean Reardon, Professor of Poverty and Inequality at

Stanford University. Instead of looking only at individual schools, he looks at school districts. He and a team of researchers spent upwards of four years putting just about all school districts onto a common scale that allows for a comparison between districts based on the socioeconomics of the students in the districts and their academic achievement. And, similar to Coleman's finding more than fifty years ago, Reardon has found that poverty and low achievement are tightly correlated: as the percentage of poor students in a district increases, academic achievement tends to decrease. There are exceptions, but that is the general tendency.

In the fifty years between Coleman and Reardon, of course, we've seen endless numbers of "reforms" aimed at breaking that correlation: comprehensive school reform, school consolidation, small schools, teacher evaluations, test-based accountability, charter schools, vouchers, personalized learning, and many—many—more. Despite the churn, on average the socioeconomic background of children still closely correlates with their academic achievement no matter how you measure it—test scores, graduation rates, college-going, or whatever measure you want to use.

That does not mean that there have been no successes. Quite the contrary. High school graduation and college attendance are at the highest level ever among all groups. And in terms of academic achievement, 9- and 13-year-olds improved in reading and math considerably throughout the 1970s and 1980s, with African American and Hispanic students improving the most.[7] Closing the test-score gap with white children seemed within sight until 1988, when progress stopped—right around the time school integration efforts also stalled. Gap-narrowing progress picked back up in the first decade of the twenty-first century, after which it stalled again.

Still, despite those periods of progress, it sometimes seems as if the correlation between socioeconomic status of children and academic achievement is tethered by some kind of law.

The question, of course, is why?

Coleman and Reardon's huge data sets can't answer that question.

To answer it, it is long past time to resurrect another line of research which has been largely ignored by huge sections of the education world.

BUILDING ON EFFECTIVE SCHOOLS RESEARCH

Sir Michael Rutter is probably the foremost child psychiatrist in the world, best known for work he has done on autism and with Romanian orphans after the fall of Nicolae Ceaușescu. Back in the late 1960s and early 1970s, before he was world famous, he became curious about Coleman's observation that some schools seemed to have more of an effect than others.

The problem he had—the problem everyone who wants to figure out the effect of schools has—is that it is hard to account for student background. Take two schools that both score at about the national average on an assessment. They might seem to be about the same in terms of their effect. But if the first school only enrolls students who have previously scored in the top tenth of achievement, then you might reasonably conclude it is a terrible school. If the second only enrolls students who are in the lowest tenth, you might conclude that it's a fabulous school that teaches a whole lot.

Rutter did something clever to address the problem of student background. He took advantage of the fact that there had been a previous study of thousands of elementary school children in London that had gathered enormous amounts of information, including the children's fathers' job status, their academic records, their school discipline records, and teacher observations. For the most part those children went on to one of twelve London high schools in a dismal and depressed part of London.[8]

Rutter and his team of researchers followed the students when they entered high school, controlling for all the background factors. They found that the children's academic achievement largely depended on which of those twelve schools the children attended. "The results carry the strong implication that schools can do much to foster good behavior and attainments, and that even in disadvantaged areas, schools can be a force for good."[9]

Rutter and his team wrote *Fifteen Thousand Hours*, taking the title from the fact that children are in school for roughly fifteen thousand hours over their school careers. They not only established that schools make a difference—in other words, they said schools can make kids smarter—but also did case studies of those schools that were most effective in raising student achievement, characteristics that added up to what Rutter called "school ethos."

Fifteen Thousand Hours was a careful study and, like all careful studies, was bolstered with a lot of qualifications, making it difficult to find a description of school ethos that doesn't last for pages. But in 2002 Rutter revisited the work he had done as a younger man. In his essay he summarized what the original report had said:

> The overall school organization or management features that stand out include good leadership that provides strategic vision, staff participation with a shared vision and goals, appropriate rewards for collegial collaborative working, attendance to staff needs and rewards, and effective home-school partnership.[10]

None of those things are weird or contrary to what most people in education would think sensible today. But they also don't constitute a recipe for what to do. Professional knowledge and skill are required to understand their implications and put them into practice.

Roughly at the same time Rutter was doing his research, Ronald Edmonds was also thinking about the question Coleman raised: Do some schools break the correlation between family background and achievement, and can we use their successes to learn how to make all schools more effective?

Edmonds had been an educator who—among other things—was assistant superintendent for the state of Michigan and senior assistant of instruction in New York City. He afterward served as director of Harvard's Center for Urban Studies and as an assistant professor at Michigan State University's school of teacher education.

He reanalyzed Coleman's data and identified schools in Michigan where poor children and Black children performed at least as well as middle-class and white children, calling them "effective schools" and then studied them to see what made them different.

In an article in *Educational Leadership,* he wrote: "What effective schools share is a climate in which it is incumbent on all personnel to be instructionally effective for all pupils. That is not, of course, a very profound insight, but it does define the proper lines of research inquiry."

When he spelled it out, his list overlapped quite a bit with Rutter's:

- They have strong administrative leadership without which the disparate elements of good schooling can neither be brought together nor kept together;
- Schools that are instructionally effective for poor children have a climate of expectation in which no children are permitted to fall below minimum but efficacious levels of achievement;
- The school's atmosphere is orderly without being rigid, quiet without being oppressive, and generally conducive to the instructional business at hand;
- Effective schools get that way partly by making it clear that pupil acquisition of basic school skills takes precedence over all other school activities;
- When necessary, school energy and resources can be diverted from other business in furtherance of the fundamental objectives; and
- There must be some means by which pupil progress can be frequently monitored. These may be as traditional as classroom testing on the day's lesson or as advanced as criterion-referenced systemwide standardized measures. The point is that some means must exist in the school by which the principal and the teachers remain constantly aware of pupil progress in relationship to instructional objectives.[11]

Edmonds died young, at the age of forty-eight. Although several people tried to continue his Effective Schools work, their efforts eventually petered out in the world of education consultancy, where they had significant effects on individual educators but less of an effect on the field as a whole.

In a 1982 interview Edmonds summed up his research approach as, "First you identify schools that produce the outcomes you're interested in. Then you watch them and try to figure out what makes them different from ineffective schools."[12]

This is such an obvious way to proceed that it seems almost self-evident. And yet, since Rutter and Edmonds, little education research has been conducted in this way. Most educational research has fallen into two categories: correlational studies a la Coleman's and Reardon's, and studies of individual practices or programs. Both kinds of research are helpful and necessary. Correlations help us keep the big picture in mind, and studies on individual programs and practices can help educators distinguish the helpful from the snake oil and discover new ways to approach problems.

But if anything is clear from the history of education it is that correlational studies don't explain why some kids don't seem to get smarter, and no single program or practice seems to make a difference. Which is to say that most educational research in the US doesn't really help schools make kids smarter, but rather describes and catalogues school failure.[13]

That said, there are exceptions. Perhaps the biggest exception is the UChicago Consortium on School Research. The Consortium was founded by Penny Sebring and Anthony Bryk, who crossed paths at Harvard with Ronald Edmonds, and whose approach to research was deeply influenced by him.

I tell the story of the Consortium in chapter 2, but essentially Consortium researchers spent twenty years studying schools in Chicago that improved and schools that didn't improve. In 2010, the Consortium published its landmark book, *Organizing Schools for Improvement: Lessons from Chicago*, which concluded that, "School organization drives improvement, and individual initiatives are unlikely to work in isolation."[14]

This might seem like a modest return on so much effort, but the implications are enormous, and they challenge what the education world has been focused on for so many years: individual programs and practices. Instead, it puts the emphasis on organizational structures and systems that work together to make kids smarter.

The UChicago Consortium researchers said that if even three of "five essentials" were in place at a high level, and if one of these was effective leadership, then schools were *ten times more likely to improve* than if they weren't in place. This was a huge finding.

What were those elements?

- Effective leaders
- Collaborative teachers
- Involved families
- Supportive environments
- Ambitious instruction

It is easy to see how the Consortium's findings dovetail nicely with Rutter's and Edmonds's. Their findings still weren't a recipe for school improvement, but they provided a bit more solid footing than educators had had before.

In response, Chicago Public Schools shifted ground. Signs went up all over the district office saying that schools were the unit of change and principals were the leaders of that change.

CPS began rating schools based on the five essentials and used surveys designed by the Consortium to gather the data. The district began focusing on ensuring that schools had principals who knew how to build school cultures where collaborative teams of teachers provided ambitious instruction and built good relationships with students and families. That's a tall order, but slowly Chicago began preparing the right kinds of principals and getting them in the right jobs.

Lots more went on in Chicago, some of which is detailed in chapter 2, but the big picture is that over three decades, the district improved. Fourth and eighth graders in Chicago now achieve at levels above many other cities and right around the national average. That is quite something for a district that was once dysfunctional enough that in 1987 then–US Secretary of Education William Bennett called it the "worst" district in the country—"an educational disaster, a complete meltdown."[15]

Many other cities have undergone massive "reform" efforts without anywhere near the improvement that Chicago schools have seen.

Serious educators pay close attention to UChicago Consortium, and several cities have recently started up their own partnerships with universities in an attempt to replicate its role in Chicago, but for the most part the Consortium's work—and the work of Chicago Public Schools as a whole—flies under the radar.

One other major piece of research is worth noting here because it falls into this same line, and that is a study by scholars at the University of Washington and University of Minnesota who studied 180 schools across eight states and six years and concluded, "We have not found a single case of a school improving its student achievement record in the absence of talented leadership."[16]

This echoed what Edmonds had said in 1982, saying that recognizing the importance of principals was "not a theory, but a discovery."[17]

All of which is to say that the failure of many of the reform efforts of the last few decades have helped feed the Coleman-derived narrative that schools can't really help kids get smarter. And, just as President Johnson seems to have feared, that has in turn fueled arguments by anti-democratic forces who are determined to starve the schools of resources in state after state. The arguments they make are not that all that different from when the white oligarchy of the South reversed the advances of Reconstruction. Schools can't make children of color and children living in poverty smarter, so why send tax money down a rat hole?

However, the Rutter-Edmonds-Leithwood–UChicago Consortium research tradition demonstrates something quite different: the knowledge of how to structure schools that make kids smarter exists. Given the right conditions, that knowledge can be exposed and learned from so that more schools can help more kids get smarter.

ABOUT THIS BOOK

This book presents the stories of five districts of widely different types—to explore the common themes among them and enable others to learn from their examples. It builds on and extends work I have done on a podcast, *ExtraOrdinary Districts*, for The Education Trust. As with the school profiles I have written, I highlight high performing and rapidly improving districts that serve students of color and students living in low-income homes who perform at high levels. Each one in some way breaks the correlation between students' background and achievement.

These are, to be sure, outlier districts. To find them, I have used a combination of Reardon's pathbreaking analyses of achievement by district and publicly available state data.

In many ways, what I have seen in each of these districts mirrors what Rutter and Edmonds found in schools decades ago, and what the UChicago Consortium continues to find in schools now.

But with school districts as the subject, the lens widens a bit. As John Daniel, superintendent of Cottonwood district in Oklahoma, says, a school district is like "a large amoeba that moves and has interlocking parts."

This book will try to describe some of those interlocking parts. It is not meant to be a guide to district administration. It is, rather, a journey through some of the nation's districts that have solved some of the problems faced by districts around the country—with insights from superintendents, principals, teachers, staff members, students, and parents.

Such a message can only really be understood within a larger political context. The belief in the capacity of schools to make kids smarter is part and parcel with a belief in the capacity of ordinary citizens to be able to govern themselves and the even more fundamental belief that all Americans are bound together equally in a common destiny.

In other words, the ideas of democracy and public schools are inextricably linked. That's hardly a new insight; Horace Mann and John Dewey both wrote eloquently on the subject, and every African American parent who put themselves and their children in grave danger in order to secure an education and their place in a democracy understood this in every sinew of their being. But right now, when antidemocratic forces have gained enormous political strength, it seems important to once again point out that democracy and public schools share a common fate. Weaken one and the other will wither.

This book is the story of people who have spent their lives and careers strengthening both.

CHAPTER 1

The Importance of Districts

When I tell people that I write about high performing and rapidly improving schools and districts that serve children of color and children from low-income backgrounds, they often ask me what the secret is.

They expect schools with those demographics to have low achievement, so they assume they must employ some kind of magic.

"They teach the kids," I say.

I know that's not really a satisfying answer, but it's easier than saying, "They organize themselves to teach all kids."

That would really confuse people. What else would schools be organized to do besides teaching kids?

What most people don't realize is that schools are organized around a lot of things. Lunch, for one. Bus schedules. Tourism.[1] Football. Schools are organized around a lot of priorities, some more important than others. Teaching and learning has to fit in.

When it comes to actual instruction, most schools organize themselves around individual teachers in classrooms. That is, students are assigned to teachers who are responsible for teaching them. Many teachers are handed the keys to their classroom and told, "Good luck!"

That organizational model, where students are dependent on their individual teachers, and individual teachers are almost solely dependent on the knowledge and skill they bring to the job, will inevitably fail vast numbers of children. That's not because teachers aren't working hard. Most are. It's because no individual teacher is capable of having all the expertise necessary to teach all children everything necessary all the time.

In order to teach all children, schools need to bring the full power they have as institutions to bear. That means that, among other things, teachers need to collaborate and learn from each other's expertise, and principals need to be able to deploy resources such as special education services, counselors, and so forth in a seamless way.

Because most schools are not set up to really foster that kind of deep collaboration, schools fail and children flail.

At bottom, in order to continually improve instruction, teachers need to be able to ask what I call the most powerful question in education: "Your kids are doing better than mine; what are you doing?" This is a question teachers can ask of their fellow teachers, but it travels up the profession; principals can ask other principals; superintendents can ask other superintendents; even governors and state commissioners of education can ask their counterparts in other states. The question can be asked about graduation rates, attendance rates, reading proficiency—anything we think is important.

Anyone who asks that question is demonstrating the necessary professional distance of someone who can look honestly at what they have been trying to accomplish and say, "Boy, I thought I was doing a great job, but most of my kids aren't doing as well as yours—what did you do?" That question is the beginning of solving a problem and improving practice.

But in order to ask that question, a lot of things need to be in place:

- A culture of trust. A teacher, principal, superintendent, or secretary of education who admits to failure should be celebrated for the vulnerability they have shown. In too many settings they are liable to be seen as incompetent rather than as highly professional.
- A common understanding of what kids need to learn and how to ascertain whether they have learned it, whether it takes the form of a quiz or a report or state assessments.
- A common schedule for when to assess.

- A common way to report the resulting data.
- Common time to look at the data and reflect on it to see where the expertise lies that needs to be learned from.

To take it back to the classroom teacher level, if teachers on a grade level all look at the results of a quiz given to all students at a grade level, one teacher might be able to see that only 25 percent of her students answered the questions correctly while 75 percent of another teacher's students did. The first teacher can say, "Your kids are doing better than mine. What are you doing?"

Then, ideally, the first teacher could go see what the second teacher is doing. Or he or she can bring the class to the second teacher. Or maybe the second teacher can go teach a lesson in the first teacher's classroom. There are a lot of solutions to the problem of how to learn from expertise. But first you have to organize the work in order to permit expertise to be able to be exposed so that it can be learned from.[2]

At the school level, principals are the people who have the power to organize in those ways.

Principals hold the power of setting master schedules, for example, which is how teachers get the kind of time to collaborate that is needed. They also organize school budgets, teacher and staff recruitment, hiring, and induction, and all the systems that allow teachers to continually learn to make better and better decisions about the instruction they provide children. I wrote about the power that principals have in *Schools That Succeed: How Educators Marshal the Power of Systems for Improvement*.[3]

But here's the thing. Most principals are not really prepared to organize schools in ways that ensure teacher and thus student success.

Quick story: A few years ago, I was visiting a truly wonderful school in Miami. It served students primarily from low-income backgrounds, most of them recent immigrants from the Caribbean and Central America. The school outperformed the state on a number of measures, and classrooms were buzzing hives of reading, writing, and academic conversation. At one point I was surrounded by a group of teachers who proudly told me how well they worked together and said that they were "like a family." Out of earshot of the principal, I asked them how long it would take for a bad principal to tear the school apart. I genuinely expected them to answer that they wouldn't permit that to happen, that they would drive a bad principal out. Instead, the answer was immediate and nearly choral.

"Twenty minutes."

They explained that any of them could immediately get a job elsewhere; they were highly sought-after by other schools, and they had no intention of ever working in a dysfunctional one. Some of them had had that experience and had no desire to do so again. They knew that their success as teachers depended on the principal setting the conditions under which they worked—the culture of trust, the coherent ways to use time and money and make decisions, and the systems of communicating both within the school and with parents and community members. A bad principal—or even just a mediocre principal—could rip all that apart and leave them to be unsuccessful. And no one wants to be an unsuccessful teacher, certainly not once they taste success.

That experience not only confirmed for me how important principals are, it made clear to me that teachers feel fairly powerless over district decisions about the principalship. They could wend their way through a system, but the Miami teachers did not feel they had any ability to shape that system to ensure that the district would assign a good principal to the school.

And, through the years, I have seen exactly what the Miami teachers feared. In fact, one of the criticisms of my work has been that the schools I write about don't seem to stay fixed. If success is not permanent, the argument goes, perhaps it is not real.

I have come to a different conclusion that I'll share in a moment.

First, I'll give the most extreme example of what I'm talking about. I first wrote about M. Hall Stanton Elementary in North Philadelphia in *It's Being Done*, after several visits from 2004 to 2006.[4] Stanton was surrounded by what looked like a bombed-out city, a monument to the neglect and disrepair we allow our cities to fall into.

The school itself was a sanctuary of calm, with teachers teaching and children learning. It was far from nirvana, but it had come a long way from when Barbara Adderley had first arrived as principal in 2001. Then it had been terrorized by what teachers called the "third- and fourth-grade gang wars," which sounds as if it should be funny but which, I was assured by teachers, was not. When Adderley arrived, Stanton was one of the lowest performing schools in Philadelphia, which made it one of the lowest performing schools in Pennsylvania. By the time I visited for the first time in 2004, the average student at Stanton was achieving about at the level of the average student in Pennsylvania. That represented truly extraordinary improvement.

In the middle of the 2006–7 school year, Adderley took a job as an assistant superintendent in her home town of Washington, DC, in part to be near her daughter and grandchildren. She had developed a very strong school with three people who were possible replacements for her. They had the certifications to be principal, and they were fully invested in the school and its culture. Instead of appointing one of them, the district appointed someone who had put in her time as an assistant principal in a nearby school and who immediately dismantled the systems Adderley had put in place. Gone were the regular data meetings, the student support teams, and the professional development based on individual teacher needs aligned to school goals. Gone was the collaboration and the firm but respectful treatment of students and teachers. Many of the staff fled, easily finding jobs elsewhere. Two of the three who had administrative credentials immediately became principal and assistant principal of a middle school in another district. Achievement at Stanton dropped, and student behavior was once again out of control. The district closed the school a few years later, but not before many tearful conversations between me and Adderley as she watched her pride and joy disintegrate.

Other schools had similar experiences. Graham Road Elementary School, which I wrote about in HOW It's Being Done, went from one of the lowest performing schools to one of the highest performing schools in Virginia under the leadership of Molly Bensinger-Lacy.[5] When she retired, she left in place someone who was credentialed to become principal, with a promise to mentor her through her first years. Instead the district brought in someone from outside the district. Once again much of the staff fled, and the person Bensinger-Lacy had hoped would be named principal took a job as principal at another school. Graham Road's test scores dropped precipitously, much to the extreme distress of Bensinger-Lacy. The children there are now among the lowest performing children in the state.

I could give other examples, but, honestly, it's too depressing. These are educational tragedies. But each one demonstrates that a school's performance is not about the kids. It's about the way the schools organize themselves to meet the needs of their students.

Watching great schools fall apart under ineffective and sometimes grossly incompetent leadership has deepened my appreciation for the key role effective principals play in school improvement. It has also driven home two things:

- Effective schools are not perpetual motion machines. You cannot simply get them set up, put them in motion, and watch them go. They require continual leadership to keep them going.
- You can fix schools all you want. If their districts are dysfunctional, they won't stay fixed.

Districts—that is to say, superintendents and school boards—appoint principals. If they don't fully understand what is needed to lead a school, they are liable to hire the wrong person. Of course, anyone can make a hiring mistake. But in a functional district, mistakes are corrected—a weak principal gets the support needed to become stronger or is replaced before too much damage is done. In dysfunctional districts, they are allowed to destroy opportunities for children.

Over the years, teachers and principals have told me endless stories of dysfunctional districts. Sometimes that takes the form of neglecting and underfunding the schools that serve their neediest children. I heard of one Alabama superintendent, for example, who only oversees eighteen schools. But somehow, in four years he never managed to visit the only three schools in his district that serve African American children. Or the superintendent of a large, high-poverty district where almost all the schools were low performing. He never managed to visit the one high-poverty school that was recognized by the state for its high achievement and regularly downplayed the school's achievements to his other principals.

I have also heard about many superintendents who say that all the schools need to have the same resources no matter what the needs of their students. So, two schools with 350 children will get one principal and one counselor, even if one of those schools serves mostly wealthy children and the other serves many children who are homeless.

In addition, districts will often assign their newest and least experienced principals to their highest need schools, which is basically a recipe for disaster. And disaster is what we often see in schools that serve large populations of children of color and children from low-income backgrounds. Even if the principal is ready to take on the challenge—a big if—they don't have the connections and influence their more experienced colleagues do. And so, they often get last dibs on teacher candidates and are saddled with the teachers and staff members their more connected principals have eased out of their schools. One principal of a high-need high school told me that she had successfully recruited the rare commodity of a physics teacher to her school, only to find out two days later that the district personnel office had disparaged the students at the high-need school and advised the candidate to take a job at another, wealthier, school.

An assistant superintendent of a large district who was in charge of fifty schools that were performing at the bottom of the state told me that she had worked hard to recruit an excellent principal to turn around one of the lowest performing of the schools. His efforts to build a respectful culture within the building were being undermined by an obdurate and hostile school secretary. The district personnel official advised him to put the school secretary on an improvement plan. "He didn't have time for that!" the assistant superintendent told me. She had to exert every ounce of power she had to insist that the school secretary be transferred to a higher performing school that had the capacity to help her improve.

All of this has made me appreciate the importance of school districts. I am still convinced that school improvement is primarily driven by principals who are able to marshal the full power of schools to support teachers and students. But districts have power to either support or undermine the work of principals.

This understanding led me to want to write about districts. I wanted to continue my basic operating theory, which is what Ronald Edmonds laid out decades ago: "First you identify schools that produce the outcomes you're interested in. Then you watch them and try to figure out what makes them different from ineffective schools."[6] The outcome I am most interested in is academic achievement (that is, test scores). But I was a bit daunted by the complexity of districts. There are almost fourteen thousand school districts in the country, and they don't have common anything—size, demographics, governance structures, finances, assessments, state policy environments. Just as I was thinking about how I would navigate all that to identify districts worth learning from, Sean Reardon at Stanford University saved me.

BREAKING NEWS: WE CAN NOW COMPARE DISTRICTS NATIONALLY

As I said in the introduction, Reardon is perhaps the closest intellectual descendent we have of James Coleman. Like Coleman, he uses large data sets to ask and answer big questions about education. But unlike Coleman, Reardon is looking at districts, not just schools. And, whereas Coleman had to administer achievement tests to thousands of students, Reardon can take advantage of the fact that every state already administers reading and math tests to every third through eighth grader in public school.

It took Reardon and a team of researchers years, but they have gathered data from every district in the country to be able to look at the relationship between the socioeconomic status of students and their academic achievement. The first I knew of this work was back in 2016 when the *New York Times* published an interactive scatterplot graphic similar to figure 1.1.[7] For socioeconomic status he didn't use the common data on free and reduced-price meals but rather the results from the Community Survey of the US Census.[8] This permits a much broader look—not just at family income, but also such factors as parental education level and the number of single parents who are in the district. From right to left he arrays the scatterplot of districts from richer to poorer. This has to be viewed a little bit cautiously, particularly with really small

FIGURE 1.1

Socioeconomic status and grade 3–8 achievement

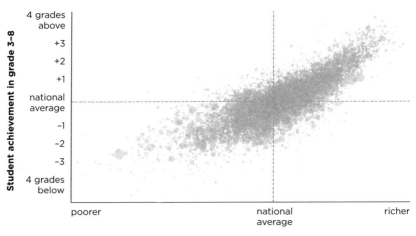

Source: Figure is based on SEDA 3.0 data (https://edopportunity.org). © sean f. reardon

districts where the survey sample may be so small as to be unrepresentative. But it gives us an idea of where districts fall.

Similarly, the way he reports academic achievement has to be used cautiously. This is because the tests that kids take in Alabama aren't really meant to be compared to the tests taken by kids in, say, Maryland. They are different tests with different achievement scales. So what Reardon did—and this also took some time—was to compare all the state assessments to the National Assessment of Educational Progress (often called the nation's report card) to report how students achieved in comparison to each other. In other words, he compared districts in Alabama to the NAEP results, and then compared districts in Maryland to the NAEP results; this allowed him to compare students in Alabama to students in Maryland. This process, called "equating," involves enough assumptions that you would never want to take two dots close to each other and say, "this district is better than that." But when you put it all together, the big picture is pretty clear: as poverty increases, academic achievement tends to decrease. That is hardly a startling finding—Coleman found that more than a half-century ago. But one of the things Reardon's analysis demonstrates vividly is that, except at the very tails of the distribution, there is enormous variation at every socioeconomic level. If you just look at the average socioeconomic level—where household income is roughly around $50,000 a year, for example—the students in Midway, Oklahoma, are scoring 1.1 grade levels above the national average; students in Adelanto, California, are at 1.8 grade levels below the national average.[9] If we were able to pull the bottom districts up to the top of their socioeconomic level, we would still have equity issues to address, but we would be in a whole different place educationally.

In any case, Reardon's analysis allows us to look for interesting outliers with "outcomes you're interested in," to use Ronald Edmonds's words, to see what kinds of things they do.

When Reardon first published his interactive scatterplot in the *New York Times,* I spent a lot of time hovering over dots, trying to figure out what might be going on in different districts. I quickly realized I had to supplement his chart with a lot of other data from state web sites. For one thing, even though he updates the data, it is never completely current. But also, there is only so much he can capture in one chart. He is not capturing improvement or deterioration over time, for example. For that information, you have to look at the district report cards on the web sites of state departments of education.

So I picked out a few outlier districts to find out more about and plumbed the depths of the state web sites in order to decide which to visit.

I ended up with a set of districts that I had identified through a bunch of numbers. And each time I visited one, I found an enormous wellspring of knowledge, expertise, and passion that we can all learn from.[10]

This has cemented my belief that one of the main reasons for all the data that we are collecting by giving kids tests—every year from third through eighth grade and once in high school—is to expose expertise so that we can learn from it.

Of course, the public has a right to know how the schools are doing, and that kind of public accountability is important. But accountability is a cudgel that has not proven particularly effective in school improvement. It has sometimes spurred educators to learn from expertise, but too often it has led to educators finding excuses for their low achievement. The really powerful way to use data is not as a shaming exercise but as an investigative exercise. And that requires stripping ourselves of our biases.

For example: Way back when I first started visiting high performing and rapidly improving schools that served children of color and children from low-income families, I began with a bit of a personal bias toward small schools. To me, the proponents of small schools had a point that small schools permitted a more personal approach so that children wouldn't find themselves as lost as they can be in large schools.

But I concentrated on finding schools solely through achievement data and demographics, and that yielded finds of large schools that did well by their students. And the more schools I visited, the more I realized that kids can feel lost and abandoned in small schools and supported and connected in large schools. The underlying problem of ensuring that every student is seen, noticed, appreciated, and taught can be solved in both large schools and small schools. Specific solutions might look a little different because of school size and resources, but successful schools will have systems to address the issue of ensuring that all children feel connected and supported.

That was a lesson for me to not have those kinds of prejudices, but to instead think about the underlying problems that face all schools and see how different schools solve them within their individual context. Because, let's face it, all schools have the same basic issues. Every school has kids who misbehave, for example. Every school has children who have difficulty learning to read. And so on. The interesting thing is to see how effective schools face those issues and how they examine their successes and failures to continually improve.

The same thing is true of districts. They all face the difficulty of ensuring that their curricula and textbooks are of high quality. They all face the difficulty of ensuring that their schools are led by principals who understand the job.

The interesting thing is to see how effective districts like the ones profiled in the following pages face those issues and how they examine their successes and failures to continually improve.

CHAPTER 2

The Work of a Generation

The Story of Chicago, Illinois

C hicago is a big city with a big story.
A story of institutional fragility and institutional resilience. A story of community engagement and investment. A story of a city with a unique history that nevertheless holds universal lessons about how, with the right kinds of information and systems of support, educators can improve instruction and students can get smarter.

First, let me tell you why I'm talking about Chicago at all.

Chicago Public Schools is one of the few districts in the country that "grows" students six academic years in five calendar years. That is to say, in Sean Reardon's initial analysis of test scores from 2009 to 2015, the average third grader in Chicago was more than a grade level behind the national average; but the average eighth grader was pretty much at the national average.[1] No other large or even medium-sized district can boast that its students improve that much from third through eighth grade.

When Reardon first unveiled this analysis in 2017, he shocked the education research world. Few expected a city where 89 percent of students are children of color and 80 percent come from low-income backgrounds to be among the top 5 percent of the nation in elementary school gains. On videos of his talks you can hear audible gasps of disbelief when Reardon got to this part. Sometimes Reardon would say something like, "I know, I didn't believe it either, but I reran the data and it said the same thing."

27

But no one should have been surprised; his analysis was merely a confirmation of other information that had been floating around for years.

Chicago is particularly data rich. In terms of test score data, not only do we have the state assessment data that Reardon uses, but we also have the NAEP TUDA data. Let me unpack that a little for non-insiders. NAEP is the National Assessment of Educational Progress, otherwise known as the nation's report card. The Main NAEP assesses the reading and math achievement of a large sample of fourth and eighth graders every two years in each of the states and some jurisdictions (like the District of Columbia and Puerto Rico).[2] Twenty-one cities and large districts participate in NAEP as if they were states. This is called the Trial Urban District Assessment (TUDA). NAEP provides clear information about how well—or how badly—students perform. It is unconnected to any kind of accountability, so no one prepares for NAEP, and the National Assessment Governing Board selects a sample of students and administers the test. So there really is no question of cheating. Even anti-test people respect NAEP.

Chicago has participated since 2002, and it improved more or less steadily until 2015, after which reading dropped a bit and math stayed steady.

Once far below the average of other TUDA districts, Chicago now matches or exceeds many other large jurisdictions, and it is near the national average for all students.

Here's a data point that I think is particularly telling: In 2011, 48 percent of Chicago's fourth graders met basic standards for reading. Four years later, 67 percent of that *same cohort of students* met basic reading standards in eighth grade.[3] Not that that's where Chicago should be. Just about all students should be meeting basic reading standards. But the fact that so many more of the same cohort of students met basic standards in eighth grade than in fourth points to what Sean Reardon found in his analysis—Chicago's kids advance academically as they go through school. No other urban district that participated in NAEP had that kind of increase from fourth to eighth grade in that period of time.

I should say that Chicago's stagnation since 2015 on NAEP means that the latest cohort's improvement isn't quite as dramatic. Fifty-eight percent of fourth graders read at least at a basic level in 2015, 63 percent of eighth graders in 2019. That still shows growth, but less than the previous cohort. On the other hand, in 2015 only 2 percent of the fourth graders read at an advanced level; in 2019, 7 percent of eighth graders were advanced. Although still a low number, that's actually really impressive, because nationally only 4 percent of eighth-grade students score at advanced levels.

But NAEP isn't all the information we have. From 2006 to 2018, high school graduation improved from 57 percent to 76 percent—81 percent if you include the alternative schools. And almost half of high school graduates enroll immediately in a four-year college and another 22 percent in a two-year college. This makes Chicago's college-going rates higher than the rest of the nation.[4]

And then, of course, we have the state assessment data that Reardon uses for his analyses. (See figure 2.1.) Student achievement in reading and math has been improving, and by 2015 almost every demographic group

FIGURE 2.1

Socioeconomic status and grade 3–8 achievement growth

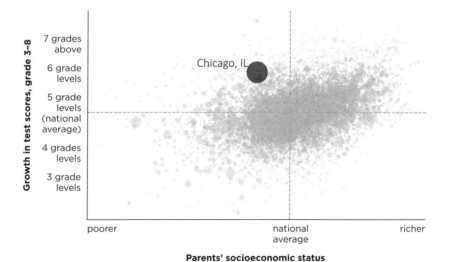

Parents' socioeconomic status

Source: Figure is based on SEDA 3.0 data (https://edopportunity.org). © sean f. reardon

in the city was outperforming its demographic group in the state. That is to say, higher percentages of white students in Chicago were meeting standards than white students in Illinois. Black students in Chicago outperformed Black students in Illinois, and so forth.[5] In 2017 the University of Illinois at Chicago's Center for Urban Education Leadership documented that although Illinois as a whole was holding steady, Chicago's gains were masking declines in the rest of the state.[6]

When I talked with Jesse Sharkey in 2017, when he was vice president of the Chicago Teachers Union—he is now president—he said he didn't know any teacher his age or younger whose children didn't attend Chicago Public Schools. When he arrived in Chicago in the late 1990s it was the exact opposite—he didn't know a teacher whose children attended the city schools.

All of which is to say that Reardon's analysis shouldn't have been a surprise—a lot of data all pointed in the same direction.

There is an important conversation to have about why people were surprised and why, even years after his analysis, you probably still haven't heard about Chicago's improvement.[7]

Part of it, I suspect, is that the nation has been conditioned to think that no good news can come out of Chicago—or any big city, for that matter. Maybe there is another country that has permitted its major cities to fall into the kind of disrepair and disrepute that Buffalo, Philadelphia, St. Louis, Detroit, and many more fell into in the 1970s, 1980s, and 1990s, but I don't know it. Chicago was no different.

You name the issue and Chicago—and Chicago Public Schools—experienced it.

NO PLACE TO GO BUT UP

Redlining, real-estate steering, hostile white neighbors, housing covenants, and racist police policies ensured that African American and Hispanic residents for the most part lived in segregated neighborhoods and that their children attended segregated—and woefully underresourced—schools. The state's school financing formula horribly underfunded Chicago schools. And all that was layered on top of the standard dysfunction of public schools, meaning they were too often badly led and haphazardly staffed.

By 1987, things were at a crisis level. A nineteen-day teacher strike seemed to be the final blow, particularly since it was the ninth strike since 1969.

Harold Washington, who had been elected mayor in 1983 partly on a wave of dissatisfaction about the schools, called a citywide summit. A thousand people showed up, and there was a lot of unhappiness and some yelling. Many Black and Hispanic parents said their children were being treated unfairly by a racist school system. Many Black teachers agreed and said that they, too, were treated unfairly by that system. Others complained about an unaccountable central office. And business people said they couldn't hire Chicago's graduates because too few could be counted on to be able to read and compute well or to have met any kind of academic standards.

Shortly afterward, then–secretary of education William Bennett flew into Chicago and pronounced Chicago Public Schools the "worst" school system in the country. He was only saying in a more brutal way what Chicagoans had been complaining about for years. But his words reverberated through the city, complete with blaring headlines and a quick search through the data in school board headquarters to try to refute him.

Then–*Chicago Sun-Times* reporter Linda Lenz reported that when Bennett returned to Washington he asked his deputy, Chester A. Finn, whether he was right to call Chicago the worst. Finn scratched his head and said something to the effect of "Close enough."[8] Certainly other cities were in contention. In fact, Bennett later told a Washington audience with much amusement that almost as soon as he returned from Chicago he got a call from the Chicago mayor's office saying that "Chicago's not the worst; Detroit's the worst."[9]

Bennett's solution to what he said was an intractable problem was to give every parent a check for $4,500 a year and let them get the best education they could buy.

Chicago chose another path, one that required a coming together by the entire community—business leaders, civic leaders, parents, community organizations, philanthropies, and universities. In so doing, it demonstrated that public institutions—even large, unwieldy ones—can improve.

One of the things to keep in mind is that Chicago—the city of Jane Addams, Ida B. Wells, and John Dewey—has a rich history of community organizing and educational scholarship. Harold Washington, the city's first African American mayor, ran against the Daley political machine as part of that history of community activism. Jesse Jackson's PUSH organization was based in Chicago, and Chicago is where community organizer Saul Alinsky developed his Rules for Radicals. The Chicago Teachers Union is Local 1 of the American Federation of Teachers, meaning it was the birthplace of the union. And for years before 1987, education researcher G. Alfred Hess had been documenting Chicago's sky-high dropout rate and its systemic misuse of federal school funds.[10]

So what happened next did not happen out of the blue, but was built on a very particular intellectual and political legacy.

Shortly after Bennett's visit to Chicago, Harold Washington died suddenly of a heart attack. But the process he had begun continued, and community leaders came together to push for the Chicago School Reform Act, passed by the state legislature in 1988. The act created local school councils for every one of the then-542 schools in Chicago. Henceforth, every school would have an elected school board consisting of six parents, two community members, and two teachers. High schools have a student member.[11] The councils had and continue to have three major tasks:

- Hire and fire the principal
- Approve the school improvement plan
- Allocate the school's Title I budget and any grant money the school secures

The School Reform Act was an attempt to break the grip of the central office by depriving it of the patronage appointments of principals and dispersing the city's huge Title I budget to the schools. The law's bet on hyperlocal control of schools was greeted with enormous skepticism. It was hard for some to see how the people who were yelling at that thousand-person summit could channel their anger into the bureaucratic structures of school governance. The next year, 227,622 votes were cast for 17,256 candidates competing for 5,420 seats, and the great experiment began.[12]

It didn't take long before the question arose: Would this help schools improve? If so, how would anyone know?

Remember, this was before what could be considered the Era of Data. Since the No Child Left Behind iteration of the Elementary and Secondary School Act passed in 2001, we have had assessment data reported not only by schools and districts but also by grade and demographic group. Assessment data doesn't provide all the information people should know, but it does shed light on whether schools are teaching children—including which groups of children—to read and do math.

But back in 1988 the only data that was being gathered nationally was the Long-Term NAEP, which tests national samples of students but isn't even broken out by state, much less by jurisdiction or school. Jurisdictions published graduation and dropout data, but every state had a different definition of what those were, so it was hard to compare across borders.[13] The college entrance exams, SAT and ACT, yielded some data. But back then they were given only to students aspiring to attend selective colleges—a small subsection of high schoolers. Actually, it was graduation and ACT data that Bennett used to justify his statement that Chicago was the worst district in America. Fewer than half of Chicago's students were graduating, and of those students who took the ACT, Bennett said half of them scored in the lowest 1 percent of the nation's test takers.

By the way, Illinois later began giving the ACT to all students, and for many years Chicago's gains outpaced the state's. All high school juniors in Illinois now take the SAT, and the average combined score for Chicago students in 2019 was 946. With poverty levels substantially above state and national averages, Chicago's SAT scores are just a bit under the state and national average.

But back to 1989.

The theory behind radical decentralization was this: "We thought that if we could get restrictive bureaucracy off the top of the local schools, school people would know what to do and would, in fact, do the things necessary to help students learn a great deal."[14]

In other words, it seemed like a good idea.

But was it?

Wanting to answer that question led to a unique feature of Chicago's story: a set of intense, professional observers, consisting of journalists and researchers, who followed the story for decades.

BETTER INFORMATION; BETTER DECISION-MAKING

Let's talk about the journalists first.

Linda Lenz, the longtime, highly respected education reporter at the *Chicago Sun-Times*, developed an idea for a specialized publication that would do nothing but cover the Chicago schools in the wake of the reform bill. She pitched the idea to the Community Renewal Society, a century-old, faith-based organization that published the *Chicago Reporter*, begun in 1972 to document the role race played in the city after the heyday of the civil rights movement. Its board agreed that school reform needed its own publication. They took the proposal to two major Chicago philanthropies—the John D. and Catherine T. MacArthur Foundation and the Joyce Foundation.

"We knew that the newspapers would have nowhere near as much of an interest in doing the kind of in-depth writing about what was going on," said the then–senior program officer for MacArthur, Peter Martinez. "We all kind of agreed this kind of magazine should be created in order to do this kind of reporting."[15]

The result was a specialized publication, the *Catalyst Chicago*, that launched in 1990 and lasted twenty-five years, until Lenz's retirement, at which point it was folded into the *Chicago Reporter*. *Catalyst* was brutal. It documented dirty buildings and professional malfeasance, drooping test scores and staff turnover, teacher shortages, exclusionary discipline, and overcrowding. The fact that *Catalyst* relentlessly covered bad news meant that when it did publish good news, it was more believed than the easily discredited press-release-puffery of the school system and the mayor's office.

But news coverage is not all it did. *Catalyst* also translated the research and findings of the second set of professional observers—the University of Chicago Consortium on School Research. Although *Catalyst* was aimed primarily at parents and community members, it became a must-read source of information for principals and many teachers, who found its plain-English explanations helpful. In this way, *Catalyst* helped educators throughout Chicago become fluent in research that might otherwise have seemed intimidating and distant and helped build a common language and vocabulary throughout the city about schools and education.

So now let's talk about the University of Chicago Consortium on School Research.

Right around the time that the reform bill was passed, Anthony Bryk arrived at the University of Chicago. Bryk had been trained at Harvard, where he had crossed paths with Ronald Edmonds, who had had considerable influence on how he thought about schools and research.[16] Bryk would go on to become widely acknowledged as an education research superstar—he recently stepped down as head of the Carnegie Institute for Teaching and Learning—and in 1990, together with Penny B. Sebring, he put together a plan to do a long-term study of the effects of the 1988 reforms.[17]

The Consortium looked to the same place *Catalyst* had looked: Peter Martinez at the MacArthur Foundation.[18]

Martinez occupies an interesting role in this story. He had been a part of the community organizing network of Saul Alinsky, and before going to the foundation had headed the Latino Institute, which represented the Latino businesses within the Chicago business community that was pushing for school improvement.

Martinez was poised, both from his position at the MacArthur Foundation and as part of the larger Chicago philanthropic community, to fund the Consortium.

"There were seventeen foundations at the time here in the city of Chicago that were heavily involved in this whole grassroots effort to bring about the school reform," he told me. "And the three biggest ones would have been the MacArthur Foundation, the Chicago Community Trust, and the Joyce Foundation. And then in addition to them there were another fourteen foundations of smaller caliber. All of those people have representatives on a single committee that met on a regular basis . . . with the academic community and the grassroots community and the business community to talk about what would need to be done to move all of this stuff forward."

In 1993 these philanthropic efforts were supplemented by almost $50 million from the Annenberg Foundation. This was part of a $500 million Annenberg Challenge, which was the largest gift to public education ever.[19] The Annenberg Foundation required localities to provide matching funds, but otherwise put few restrictions on how the money was spent. Its theory was that if schools had more money they would know how to improve student achievement. For the most part, the Annenberg Challenge was considered a bit of a bust, including in Chicago.[20] But it provided hundreds of Chicago schools with some money to try different things, which provided researchers with yet another variable to study.

But one of the things that Martinez insisted on was that the research he funded wouldn't just be research for research's sake.

"I had extensive conversations with Tony [Bryk] at that point about this has got to be the kind of research that is useful to community groups and practitioners, not to academic priorities," Martinez said.[21] "Their studies had to tell us something that was useful and that would help the community and practitioners do something about improvement."

Martinez wanted the Consortium to not only describe what was going on in Chicago Public Schools, but to explain why and point to solutions.[22]

"Researchers will say to you, 'Well you know the only way we can get into that is we're going to have to do case studies, and that's going to cost us.'" Martinez said that Bryk told him, "We don't have the money to do that kind of thing. So, we can tell you what the situation is. We can't always tell you why it is that way."

It wasn't that Bryk resisted the idea of digging deeper, Martinez said. Rather, he was saying, "'In order for us to do this in a credible way, it's going to cost a lot more money.'"

Martinez had the way to break that logjam: "We gave them more money."

And thus began what is arguably the most important school research project in the country. "There's nothing like it anywhere," Bryk told me. "It was really a focus on what kind of information might actually help people get better at their work."

First off, Bryk and Sebring assembled a set of education research superstars. "We assembled some of the best applied social scientists—education researchers who we thought knew something about the organization of schools around student learning, professional development of teachers, what was happening to urban youth—and who wanted to see their future as bringing a high quality analytic and empirical orientation to actually solving education problems," Bryk said. "We brought an analytic and empirical discipline to the work."

They had what Bryk calls a "second pillar" to their work, which was actually trying to do things that would improve schools, not just study them. Bryk and Sharon Greenberg had started the Center for Urban School Improvement that was the center of that work. "We were out in schools literally every day, working in some of the most disadvantaged school communities in Chicago," Bryk said. And all the time they were studying the effects of their work and listening to those who were in the schools. "The lifeblood of the work is the voices of teachers, principals, and school community leaders who are actually trying to make their schools better."

None of this was quick or easy. There were fits and starts and difficult conversations with district officials who weren't always happy with the Consortium's findings. They rarely made for good press releases.

In fact, Mayor Richard Daley Jr., impatient with the lack of clear improvement in test scores, got a second reform bill passed through the state legislature in 1995 that gave him full control over appointing the citywide school board and the superintendent. This gave Chicago a unique governance structure that is radically decentralized for some purposes and highly centralized for others.

Daley began with a barn burner as his first school appointment. Paul Vallas had been Daley's budget director. He wasn't a professional educator and didn't have the certification necessary to be superintendent, so Daley convinced the legislature to create the position of Chief Executive Officer to head the schools. It's hard to find anyone who thinks Vallas really understood education or schools, but he is widely credited for straightening up CPS's finances and beginning a massive building and renovation project to modernize the schools. He shook up the bureaucracy and began leading it into what was soon to be the twenty-first century. When Vallas left in 2001, Mayor Daley appointed one of Vallas's deputies, Arne Duncan, to be CEO.

Duncan's tenure, which lasted until 2009, when he became President Barack Obama's secretary of education, was marked by a few things. First, stability. From 1995 to 2009 Chicago had only two CEOs, and they were able to wield enough resources and collaboration that Chicago had no teacher strikes the entire time, in marked contrast to the years before and since.

Duncan also enthusiastically partnered with some in the business community—particularly hedge fund managers—who had decided the path forward was to create new schools, both charter and noncharter. Over the next decade, one hundred new schools were created, many of them charters. In an analysis Reardon did, as well as in other's studies, the charters more or less mirrored the traditional district schools in their performance.[23]

Duncan appointed as his chief education officer Barbara Eason-Watkins, a longtime, highly respected principal who knew the system well.[24] She led a huge effort to improve instruction, including bringing in nationally known and respected reading researcher Timothy Shanahan as director of literacy. Shanahan launched the Chicago Reading Initiative, which trained and sent reading specialists to 114 schools where two-thirds or more of the students read below grade level to help teachers understand how to teach all the elements of reading, a topic insufficiently covered in most teacher training programs.

Eason-Watkins also marshaled the resources to counter a problem that had emerged as a result of the federal 2001 No Child Left Behind reauthorization of the Elementary and Secondary Education Act. NCLB required that every classroom have what it called a "highly qualified teacher." This requirement ran afoul of Chicago's system of K–8 grammar schools, which had departmentalized their upper grades so that students had math teachers, history teachers, and so forth. For the most part the teachers who had taught in the upper grades had generalized K–8 certificates, which meant they did not have the certification that would allow them to be considered "highly qualified" to teach a specific secondary subject. The schools were forced to return to self-contained classrooms where teachers taught all subjects.

The Chicago Community Trust—one of the biggest Chicago philanthropies—spent $5 to $8 million a year for ten years to create credentialing and endorsement programs at local universities for teachers in math, science, reading, and history so that teachers could teach secondary subjects and schools could reestablish departmental structures. This meant, for example, that students could take algebra in eighth grade. Terry Mazany, who for many years headed the Chicago Community Trust and also serves on the board of the National Assessment Governing Board, which administers NAEP, credits this program with the improvement of Chicago's students as they progress from fourth to eighth grade. "That was a ten-year investment to build teacher capacity," he said.[25]

One of the most important things Duncan did was to deepen the district's commitment to gathering and using data. So, for example, Vallas initially signed up to participate in TUDA, but it was first administered under Duncan. Participating in TUDA is an act of bureaucratic courage; TUDA results are unsparing and rarely make for good press coverage. They certainly didn't in those early years, with results way below those of other cities. Duncan also tightened the relationship between CPS and the UChicago Consortium by signing a data-sharing agreement that meant that researchers had access to just about all the data in the system, including attendance, high school transcripts, and state testing data. This kind of data sharing is a researcher's dream and meant that lots of questions could be asked and answered about the effect of programs, people, and practices.

Meanwhile, back at the UChicago Consortium, researchers had spent ten years studying the effect of the local school councils, and in 1998 they published *Charting School Reform: Democratic Localism as a Lever for Change*.[26]

The enormously careful study found, in the words of one of the authors, John Q. Easton, "Decentralization kind of spurred some improvement but it was pretty much unequally distributed across the system." That is to say, this behemoth of a school system, with four hundred thousand students, had improved. But there was a big *but*. The most vulnerable of the system's students—African American students and students in schools where poverty was most concentrated—had for the most part been left out of the improvement. "Improvements were more likely to occur in slightly more advantaged schools and more racially integrated schools," Easton said.[27]

Mind you, by this time white flight had left Chicago with a student body where more than eighty percent of the students were students of color, mostly African American but with a substantial and growing Hispanic population, mostly from Puerto Rico and Mexico. Also, 80 percent of the children met the qualifications for the federal free and reduced-price meal program. So there weren't a lot of wealthy schools or even all that many racially integrated schools. But certainly, some schools had much more entrenched and concentrated poverty and racial isolation than others, and they were among the schools that were left furthest behind.

That was the correlational part of the study. They dug in a little further below those big averages and found that there were a bunch of schools that were very similar in all the external, measurable factors—size, demographics, resources—that performed quite differently. Some had improved a lot and some not at all.

The question was why?

That was answered by case studies which found, in Bryk's words, "When the people at the school building level were able to work effectively together, and there was a strong relational trust—as we called it—that developed among the professionals with parents and with community, that those local actors working together were actually able use the resources they had to make their school work better. It very much taps into this idea that people engaged in the work were central to the improvement."

That may not sound all that revolutionary but this was at a time when school improvement efforts nationally were largely being directed at developing, testing, and evaluating programs that, in the phrase that is still popular, could be "scaled up" by having them be adopted by schools and districts. Bryk characterized those kinds of efforts as: "There is a small group of 'better-knowers,' whether it's policy analysts or people in positions of elected authority, and they're going to tell everybody else what to do. Well, organizations don't typically get better that way."[28]

Studying the LSCs had gotten the Consortium researchers into schools and observing how they worked in great detail, which had yielded some intriguing observations about schools and how they get better. But these were just baby steps.

Much of the city was focused on the terrible dropout rates that meant that only about half of students graduated. The assumption among many educators and others had been that students dropped out because of difficult personal circumstances such as pregnancy or incarceration and poor academic preparation. But when Consortium researchers dug into the data it showed something different—that many students who dropped out had been doing fine until ninth grade. Test scores and personal circumstances couldn't really predict who would drop out.

A breakthrough came with a 2007 paper authored by Elaine Allensworth and John Q. Easton, *The On-Track Indicator as a Predictor of High School Graduation.*[29] They found that you could predict with a lot of accuracy whether a student would drop out by their attendance and course grades—data that could be gathered from the first weeks of high school and even back in middle school. They also found that different schools had dramatically different dropout rates even when they had very similar student populations. "This suggests that school climate and structure play a significant role in whether students succeed in high school," Allensworth and Easton wrote.[30]

The 2007 report hit Chicago high schools like a slow-moving freight train. It turned out that students dropped out for a whole host of reasons—including difficult personal circumstances—but in many cases they simply felt lost and not part of school.

"I didn't know those things," said Chicago Teachers Union president Sharkey, who was a high school teacher back then. "I'm an Ivy League–educated guy, I was in a teacher preparation program, and I felt like I was pretty well prepared. And then suddenly we're all having professional development where everyone's talking about how to measure freshman-on-track and what that means."

Educators began trying different things to get students on track—phone calls home, tutoring sessions, counseling, matching students with mentors, Saturday school, summer bridge programs—all kinds of things. Some efforts were successful, some not, and the stories of success and failure spread through the city—both formally through networks of high schools that were set up to talk through problems of practice, and informally as teachers and principals transferred from school to school. In that way, educators learned from their peers what was working and under what conditions—and what wasn't.

"You do that over a number of years, and it takes a while to see it, but it has had an effect," said Sharkey.[31]

In 2010 CPS began providing principals with lists of students who had multiple absences or failing grades after the first quarter and in monthly reports after that. This was information that had always been available to principals, of course, but providing them with the lists of names made it easy for principals to act even if they weren't comfortable digging through data. That year, the graduation rate jumped from 60 to 64 percent and has crept up ever since, sitting at 77.8 percent in 2019. That's still not good enough, of course. But it is a long way from where it was.

Allensworth later wrote, about the effect of all of this work, "When high school dropout is viewed as a problem rooted in the struggles of individual children, it is an impossible problem to solve. When viewed as a problem of the design of schools as systems, it becomes solvable— if time and resources available for intervention are commensurate with the level of need across schools. Multiple systems for monitoring and intervention together potentially could dramatically reduce dropout and increase rates of high school graduation."[32]

Janice Jackson, who is at this writing the chief executive officer of Chicago Public Schools, was a high school principal then. "I led a high school prior to freshmen on track being a major metric that we use to track our success and also led it afterwards. And I can tell you that it was one of the key changes in my practice."[33]

Part of the reason it was so powerful, she said, was that she and other principals could see a clear pathway forward through the forest of principals' gargantuan to-do lists to focus on something that actually improved student success. "It really empowered us, because oftentimes when you work in schools [the job] feels insurmountable."

This is one of the reasons that Elaine Allensworth, current director of the UChicago Consortium, defines her job as helping educators understand "what to focus on," as she puts it. "A lot of times there actually isn't good data for the things that people think they have data on or that they think are important." For example, she says that many educators focus closely on test scores. That close focus, she says, doesn't actually lead to big improvements in test scores, let alone anything else. "But what we see is when students actually start coming to class and being more engaged in their classes, which means they're getting higher grades, feeling challenged, and getting support, we see improvements *not only in test scores* but also in their grades and graduation and college readiness."

Rather than focus on state assessment scores—which are reported once a year and are thus difficult to act on in a timely way—Allensworth says educators would do much better to focus on attendance. "If you could get students coming to school every day, from everything that we've seen, that would have an enormous impact not just on overall achievement but also on equity. And yet that's something people tend not to focus on because they think oh, it doesn't really matter."[34]

The Freshman On-Track Indicator report had gone a long way to doing what Martinez had asked of the Consortium—providing information and research that would be useful to practitioners, and thus establishing itself as a real partner with the district.

SCHOOL ORGANIZATION, NOT INDIVIDUAL INITIATIVES

The next breakthrough came in 2010 when Bryk, Sebring, Allensworth, Easton, and their colleagues published *Organizing Schools for Improvement: Lessons from Chicago.*[35] Using fifteen years of data, they identified one hundred schools that had improved and one hundred similar schools that had not. From the outside, many looked identical in terms of demographics, staffing, and funding. In fact, the prologue provides profiles of two schools only two miles apart, both serving low-income African American neighborhoods and sharing many characteristics. Each had principals who cared deeply about improvement, but one school improved enormously while the other stagnated.

The rest of the book explores the difference between the improvers and the non-improvers. And what they found confirmed what Allensworth and Easton had begun to articulate with the 2007 study: *school organization, not individual initiatives, drives improvement.*

That is a simple thing to say but actually a difficult concept to grasp.

When we attend school as students — or send our children to school — we think of teachers as enormously powerful. And, of course, they are powerful. They hold the power of imparting or withholding knowledge, support, and approval. The hours teachers spend with children can have an outsized effect not only on students' learning, but on their sense of well-being and agency.

It is because of that power that much of what is known as the "school reform movement" has focused on the practices and effect of individual teachers. NCLB, for example, called on every teacher to be what it called "highly qualified." This is a difficult-to-quantify idea because degrees and certifications have never been linked to whether teachers helped students learn. To solve that problem, an economist, William Sanders, identified a measure of teacher effectiveness he called "value-added." The idea was that every student's academic growth could be graphed, much like a baby's growth chart, by using their incoming test scores and their end-of-year test scores. If you look at all the students in a teacher's class you can see if they all grow at an average rate — or at a higher or lower rate of growth. Teachers where students don't grow the way they should can be identified as ineffective, and teachers whose students grow more than average can be identified as highly effective, Sanders said.[36]

This was a transformative idea, and all around the country school reformers worked to identify effective, mediocre, and ineffective teachers. The Gates Foundation put massive amounts of money into an effort — $100 million in Hillsborough County, Florida, alone — to implement new teacher evaluation systems that would allow teachers to be sorted through both value-added measures and in-person observations. The idea was that ineffective teachers could be fired, effective ones promoted, and mediocre ones could be helped to get better. In this way, the theory went, schools would improve. Districts could also use the data to assign their strongest teachers to their neediest schools; some districts provided bonuses for highly effective teachers to go to low performing schools.

What could be called the Good Teacher/Bad Teacher hypothesis had a lot of problems, but the main one is that it doesn't account for the fact that within traditionally organized schools and districts, teachers are powerless over the systems and conditions that make their jobs doable or undoable—master schedules, professional development, budgets, staffing, curriculum, program adoption, and school culture.[37] Teachers are only one part of larger organizations whose systems and resources largely determine whether they can be successful in their teaching, and thus whether their students can be successful in their learning.[38]

It isn't really surprising that most of the experiments luring teachers who had been deemed highly effective to low performing schools fizzled—in general those teachers had small effects on overall school performance, and the teachers tended to flee as soon as the bonuses ended.[39] In fact, the entire effort of applying value-added measures to teachers was pretty much a bust. Not only that, but once assessment was tied to evaluations, a lot of teachers became hostile to the whole idea of assessment for any purpose.[40]

In essence, school reformers working on the Good Teacher/Bad Teacher hypothesis had ignored the basic insight of Edmonds and Rutter that schools, not teachers, are the unit of study, change, and improvement.

Somewhat insulated from those national discussions and immersed in its painstaking study of hundreds of schools, the Consortium had confirmed Rutter's and Edmonds's insight. It wasn't that teachers weren't important, but the individual practices of teachers alone could not drive improvement. Rather, the Consortium researchers said, schools improve as the result of people working together cooperatively over extended periods of time to develop coherent instruction and build a culture of improvement.

What was required?

- *Involved Families*: Does the school partner with families and communities?
- *Supportive Environment*: Is the school safe and supportive with high expectations?
- *Ambitious Instruction*: Is instruction focused, challenging, and engaging?

- *Effective Leaders*: Does leadership focus on results and school improvement?
- *Collaborative Teachers*: Do teachers work well together and strive for excellence?[41]

When schools had all five essentials firmly in place, they were ten times as likely to improve than if they didn't, the Consortium found. In fact, three of the five would do it, as long as one of them was an effective leader. This is an enormously consequential finding. School reform efforts at the time were searching for programs, practices, and policies that would move the needle in much more incremental ways than that. They still are. The five essentials, though, is a complicated recipe. Simply adopting a program, practice, or policy isn't enough to achieve them.

Still, once these five essentials had been identified, the really tough work could begin. The Consortium researchers developed ways to measure each of the five essentials, many of which involved careful surveys of students, teachers, and occasionally parents. Today, Chicago Public Schools reports on how strong each of those elements are in schools as part of its accountability system, along with more traditional measures like test scores and graduation rates. You can go on any of Chicago's school websites and see whether teachers report good relationships with parents, whether students feel safe in and around the school, and whether teachers regularly work with their colleagues.

A NEW FOCUS ON SCHOOL LEADERSHIP

"Effective leaders" is listed as one of the five essentials, but *Organizing for School Improvement* actually identified effective leaders as the piece that undergirds all the others. That is, none of the rest—a safe and welcoming environment, a collaborative culture, a strong relationship with parents and communities, and even rigorous instruction—is possible without an effective school principal.

School principals, the Consortium researchers concluded, are the drivers of school improvement. This might seem obvious. Certainly, teachers had always understood that principals can make or break a school. But it wasn't obvious to lots of people who were thinking about school improvement at the time. They had more or less considered principals as interchangeable middle managers rather than as leaders, and they did not see the principalship as a key role for improving student learning outcomes.

Others in Chicago had begun realizing the importance of principals from different vantage points, including Steve Tozer, professor at the School of Education at the University of Illinois at Chicago (UIC). Tozer had arrived in Chicago in 1995 from the University of Illinois at Urbana-Champaign as what he calls a "teacher quality guy." Convinced that the key to school success for children from low-income families was the quality of classroom instruction, he had focused on teachers and how they were trained. Novice teachers typically learn more about teaching in their first few years on the job than in their teacher education programs, so he decided that one potent lever of change was the mentoring of new teachers. With a grant from the MacArthur and Mc-Dougal Family Foundations, he worked for seven years to make sure that new teachers in Chicago were mentored into the profession in ways that would improve their ability to help students learn. When he studied the results, he found something he hadn't expected.

"Principals were making or breaking the money we were putting into the schools," he said. "When principals understood it, it was a success. When they didn't understand it, we may as well not have done it." Not only that, but when principals understood the importance of developing teachers, the mentoring program was superfluous because the principals were already doing what was necessary to develop new teachers.[42]

He concluded after seven years that his work was never going to make a large-scale difference. "I decided if I was serious about quality of student learning and serious about quality of instruction that I was going to have to actually start to focus on principals and school leaders as the key ingredient."

The MacArthur Foundation's Martinez was concluding much the same thing at much the same time. He had been funding reading and other programs to go into schools, but when schools didn't have a strong leader, "No matter how good [the] program is, it goes nowhere and I'm putting money down the drain. And I'm beginning to see that," Martinez said. "Steve and I began comparing notes."

Together they began with a question: is it possible to develop principals who can consistently improve student achievement in underresourced urban schools?[43]

Fifteen years later, the answer is yes, and the program they built—the Center for Urban Educational Leadership at UIC—has provided a good bit of the evidence.

The first fifteen graduating classes yielded 128 Chicago principals whose schools have, in general, led the district in test-score improvement. That is to say, Chicago schools as a whole have improved, but the schools led by UIC graduates have improved more. This is quite significant and points to the notion that principal development can be not only a school improvement strategy, but a district improvement strategy.

Along the way were a lot of struggles. Among other things, they challenged two large, balky institutions: Chicago Public Schools and the University of Illinois at Chicago.

The university came first. Knowing that putting together the kind of principal preparation program that would actually be able to make change on a systemwide scale would stretch university structures, Tozer brought Martinez into the program as codirector specifically to be what he called "a change agent," something few university professors know how to be. As Tozer puts it: "The reason we became professors was partly because we know our stuff and partly because we want the autonomy to pursue our stuff. And our stuff is typically not working to change institutions."[44]

It was, however, Martinez's stuff. He drew on his years of training community organizers. "What I knew from my background was that we had to have coaching," Martinez said. "And we had to have internships."

And, he argued, the university had to be able to select the candidates carefully. "I knew that there were certain things we couldn't train, or wouldn't have time and resources to train," he said. The program needed to attract people who already understood instruction and had demonstrated that they could lead adults. In addition, he said, "We couldn't develop drive. We couldn't develop high expectations . . . We had to get people who weren't going to use obstacles—and there were going to be plenty of obstacles—as an excuse."

It took two years just to develop the program, in part because of opposition from within the university.

Some faculty members, for example, argued that offering an EdD—widely thought of as a lesser doctorate—meant it would be a repository for African Americans who weren't good enough to get a PhD. "They said these kinds of things!" Tozer remembers. Others argued that the program would serve as a barrier to African Americans and other marginalized people from gaining power. "We were getting it from both sides," Martinez said.

Now that it has proven so successful, the UIC structure is widely regarded as being the mark of a high-quality program, and other institutions around the country are working to adopt the program's most critical elements, which are:

- *Selective enrollment.* Most principal preparation programs in the country accept any teacher who wants to enroll, and the fastest growing programs are online. As a result, states have more people credentialed to be principal than want to be principal—most are teachers seeking to get the bump in pay that accompanies a master's degree and have no desire to be administrators. UIC requires candidates to already have a master's degree and to commit to seeking a principalship upon graduation. Ninety-six percent of their graduates become principals or assistant principals within a year, most of them in Chicago.
- *Cohort model.* Cohorts of students go through the experience of classroom instruction, internships, and early years on the job together, forming their own support group and network.
- *Paid internship.* Each student completes a yearlong paid internship during which the candidate, among other things, is responsible for identifying an issue in the host school and leading change. Many districts balk at the internship. Paying a principal intern for a year when they are not actually responsible for a school strikes many superintendents and school boards as a luxury. It has proven to be key to the program's success.

- *Ongoing coaching.* Students are coached through both the internship and the first year of being a full principal. Although interns were assigned to mentor principals, Martinez and Tozer wanted someone from the university who had a record of leading schools to improved outcomes and who was dedicated solely to the development of the intern.[45]

Early on, Tozer said, "Peter had one really fundamental insight that has animated our program to this day. He said we've got to stop thinking about our clientele as graduate students who want the principal credential and start thinking about our clientele as the kid in a public school who needs a principal. It was the single most profound thought shift that we made."

By 2003 UIC had begun producing principals. But they still needed to be hired. The parents and community members who sat on local school councils didn't necessarily understand what knowledge and skills they should be looking for in a principal and routinely replaced departing principals with assistant principals—a "recipe for stagnation," as Tozer said.

So CPS began using a 1996 law that allowed it to impose a more rigorous candidate assessment for principal eligibility. The initial effort involved a two-day process with simulations and role plays with paid actors. Candidates would receive scores from trained observers that could be used by local school council members in their deliberations. Later the process was streamlined and simplified, and candidates had to pass in order to be considered by the councils.

"Prior to us having this eligibility process I think that what happened in some schools was that people maybe were not prepared for the rigors of the principalship," CEO Jackson told me. Not only did they not have the ability to run the schools but they didn't understand how to develop people. "Can you develop teachers to be high performing teachers? Can you develop parent leadership within your building? Can you develop student leadership in your building? Can you create conditions for children to be successful? We look for those types of things and attributes in folks before they are able to be in this pool that local school councils choose from."[46]

After the new eligibility assessment was put in place in 2004, something on the order of 60 percent of those with regular state administrative credentials who applied for the CPS principal eligibility pool failed. In comparison, only 10 percent of UIC graduates failed; some years, none did.

Over time LSCs hired more and more graduates of UIC and also graduates of the nonprofit group New Leaders and a few smaller programs. New Leaders and UIC alone have contributed more than 350 new principals to CPS over the past two decades. UIC has documented that the schools led by its graduates first improved the climate and culture of the schools and, slowly, the graduation rates in the high schools. Test scores improved eventually, but they were often a lagging indicator. The majority of principals who graduate from UIC's program have been African American and Latino, proving the university naysayers wrong.

By 2010 Chicago had demonstrated so much success with its approach to the principalship that UIC led a state task force that resulted in decertifying all existing principal preparation programs and only recertifying those that incorporated the key elements of selective admission, internship, and ongoing coaching.[47] This makes Illinois one of very few states that has recognized both the importance of principals and the role that state policy has in ensuring that principals are prepared to lead schools, particularly high-need schools.

Chicago has become so well known for its principals that it's become a recruiting ground for other districts in Illinois and elsewhere in the country. After 150 principals left CPS in two years in the early 2010s, the city coalesced around a new effort to not just develop a strong pipeline of principals, but to retain them as well. Together with the Chicago Public Education Fund and other city nonprofits, CPS began the Chicago Principal Partnership to identify ways to recognize and support principals so that they won't be tempted to leave the city. Every year the Fund surveys principals to ask what obstacles are in the way of doing their jobs and what support they would like. Among other things, the Fund identifies high performing principals and links them with Northwestern University, where they have access to scholars and business leaders who meet with them regularly. Principal retention has improved dramatically.

One of the interesting things about this is that the Fund began in 2000 with money left over from the Annenberg Challenge. Its board, which included then–state senator Barack Obama, had committed the organization to "one aspect of public schools, and that is great talent," in the words of Heather Anichini, its president. Initially that meant focusing on teachers and teacher quality. But as the rest of the city shifted, it too shifted its focus to principals. "What we know from the data—and we are so fortunate to have such great research here—is that good principals keep good teachers," said Anichini. "And so, making that bet on principals for us is absolutely still a bet on great teachers."[48] The Fund acts as the lead organization of a coalition of community and philanthropic organizations that have all agreed to making the principalship the center of their work.

Today, principals trained by UIC and other high-quality programs do not only lead schools around the city. Many have also gone into district leadership, serving as network and department chiefs and in other key district leadership roles. The most notable example is Janice Jackson, who first became chief education officer and then chief executive officer under Mayor Rahm Emanuel and was reappointed in 2019 by the new mayor, Lori Lightfoot.

HIGH EXPECTATIONS FOR ALL STUDENTS

Simply providing stability in the office across two mayors is an accomplishment; between Arne Duncan and Jackson, seven CEOs wandered through Chicago Public Schools. Some were interims, some momentary flash-in-the-pans, and others downright scandalous; the last two CEOs before Jackson were forced to depart for ethical violations, including one who was sentenced to prison. But Jackson is hoping to do more than simply provide stability.

"It is about creating policies and structures and expectations that are the same across the board for everybody," she said. "If we really spend time unpacking what we mean when we say the same expectations, I think it challenges a lot of the practices that we have every day. If all of us are being honest, we don't always approach every student with the same level of expectations."[49]

She gives as an example of what she means, "Learn, Plan, Succeed," the policy she announced in 2017 that every student must have a post-secondary plan before graduating. The plan might be acceptance to college or an apprenticeship program or a concrete employment plan. Some objected to what seemed to them to be yet another barrier to graduation. When a reporter asked her if she was trying to "impose middle-class values" on students, Jackson, who grew up on the South Side of Chicago in a working-class African American home and attended Chicago public schools from Head Start through the doctoral program at UIC, says she was taken aback. "At the core of it what I heard is: why are you expecting low-income, predominantly Black and Latino kids in Chicago to do what everybody else is doing throughout the United States? That's what I heard." The former teacher and principal said, "I believe everybody wants to learn, everybody wants a good education and access to the American Dream, however you define that."

Jackson is adamant that key to Chicago's improvement is its transformation of the role of the principal. "If I was giving advice to other districts, I would say pay attention to school leadership, because it can have a dramatic impact on performance in the school and the district."

As CEO, Jackson has given principals even greater ability to run their schools. So, for example, she developed a policy that guarantees a school's budget in early spring, holding them harmless for any drops in school population that may occur between the spring and the fall. To those who haven't hung around schools much that may sound technical and uninteresting. But in many districts what happens is that schools' budgets are based on a prediction of what the enrollment will be in the fall. If fewer than expected students show up, the school's budget is cut by some per-pupil amount. This means that weeks into a school year, many principals around the country are faced with cutting teaching positions. They have to make difficult choices between cutting an art teacher or a kindergarten teacher, making class sizes bigger or combining classes so that one teacher teaches third- and fourth-grade students. This kind of disruption is disastrous for school morale and continuity of instruction. And it gets worse if students show up later in the fall after the cuts are made, because even if the budget gets readjusted—which it rarely does—the laid-off teachers have usually found other jobs and the principal has to hire someone brand new. All this makes it very difficult, even for the most skilled and expert principals, to build a coherent school culture.

While providing more power and stability to principals, Jackson has recognized that the fact that every school has been allowed to choose its own curriculum has meant that all students are not held to the same standards across the city. As chief education officer she led an effort that has continued as she became chief executive officer to build a new, voluntary curriculum that would be rigorous, aligned to standards, and with a clear progression through the years. "People may agree or disagree but it's not rocket science running a school. I really believe that. I think that there are some very basic things that every good school has—a good leader . . . great teachers, and what [Robert] Marzano calls a guaranteed and viable curriculum."[50] Surveys of Chicago teachers have shown that many would like a clear coherent curriculum because they spend weeks every year searching the internet for materials for lessons instead of focusing on teaching.

All of which is to say that there are a lot of different feedback loops within Chicago Public Schools—surveys, research data, and network conversations that provide an enormous amount of information to inform decisions. The Consortium continues to provide more and more granular and detailed information about the experiences of Chicago students as they progress through the grades and enroll in college. So, for example, in 2012 they found that students who took International Baccalaureate classes in high school graduated from college at a higher rate in comparison to similar students who were not in IB classes. After that, Chicago expanded its IB programs, particularly in neighborhood nonselective high schools.

One such is Senn High School in the Edgewater area of Chicago. With demographics that more or less mirror the demographics of Chicago, including having 78 percent of students considered to be from low-income backgrounds, Senn has long had an IB program. But until recently it was only for a small, select group of students. Now the aim is to make sure more and more students at least take IB classes, even if they aren't part of the full diploma program. "We've had kids who come in our neighborhood program," principal Mary Beck said. "And by tenth grade they take full honors and by eleventh grade they're in full D[iploma] P[rogram]. There's a lot—well, not a lot—but there is movement across and we allow for that and we encourage it."[51]

Jordan Clark, who was a junior in 2017, was one of those students who moved from the neighborhood program into IB after a teacher encouraged him to enroll in honors algebra. "Coming in to the general program I noticed it, well, I guess it wasn't as rigorous as I wanted because I wanted to challenge myself." As if to demonstrate Janice Jackson's point, the young African American man said, "What I really like about [the IB program] is, strangely enough, the rigor, because the IB program allows you to expand your mind."[52]

One of the things that has to be mentioned is the demographic shift that has occurred in Chicago Public Schools. As in the 1980s, about 89 percent of students are students of color and about 80 percent qualify for free and reduced-price meals. But Hispanic students now make up 47 percent of the total student population, while African American students have dropped to about 36 percent. This is part of a larger citywide shift. Something on the order of two hundred and fifty thousand African American Chicagoans have left the city in the last two decades, and it isn't exactly clear why. Some seem to have been pushed to the Chicago suburbs and northwest Indiana when housing projects were torn down. Some have moved back to the South their parents and grandparents fled in the twentieth century.[53] It will require some careful study to understand what is happening and why, but it isn't much of a leap to guess that some families leave "because of the schools." No doubt many parents fear that Chicago Public Schools haven't improved since they themselves attended, and their impressions haven't been counteracted by any kind of sustained coverage about the improvements. Newspaper and radio stories talk about test score gains, but for the most part those occasional stories consist of man-bites-man curiosities without much explanation.[54]

And, of course, Illinois has underfunded Chicago's students for years. I should say that almost all states have inequitable school funding structures, but Illinois was for many years the most inequitable by far, meaning that Chicago's students received 75 cents for every dollar the rest of Illinois's students received. "You can't deny the fact that Chicago public schools is predominantly African American and Latino and the rest of the state is not," Janice Jackson said in 2017 after Illinois's Republican governor had spent years in an open war with Chicago. She added, "I think that that shows a value system that should not be allowed to stand."[55] The following year, with a new Democratic governor, the Illinois state legislature passed a huge new funding bill that was aimed at fixing those inequities.

The new money that began flowing didn't end strife. In 2019 the Chicago Teachers Union staged a major strike that lasted eleven days—the longest strike since that transformative one in 1987. Notably, the major issues at stake were less about teacher pay and benefits and more about class size, whether schools would have nurses and social workers, and whether teachers would have time to collaborate with colleagues. The teachers secured major concessions from the city, but there was lingering bitterness among union members over having to fight a mayor who had campaigned on such issues as nurses and social workers in the schools.

CORONAVIRUS AND THE RACIAL RECKONING

Which brings us to how Chicago has responded to two events that may usher in momentous change: the abrupt closing of school buildings in the spring of 2020 as the coronavirus swept across the nation followed by what has been called the "racial reckoning" in response to the murder of George Floyd and other African Americans by police.

Chicago was emblematic of what was seen around the country when schools shut down: the United States is built on deep inequities. So, for example, it became clear to many, some for the first time, that many children cannot count on eating regularly unless they go to school. Around the country schools mobilized to feed children even with closed buildings, and Chicago was no exception, providing millions of meals from 270 school sites through the summer. If it wasn't the biggest food program in the country it was certainly one of them.

But that was just the beginning of what needed to happen. Many families did not have access to the communication infrastructure that defines the twenty-first century. They either didn't have tablets or laptops or they didn't have reliable internet service or both. That meant students couldn't continue their schooling in the ways that affluent children could. After quickly surveying families, CPS distributed one hundred and twenty-five thousand devices and thousands of hotspots.

Huge training efforts also meant that in a matter of weeks teachers who had gone a career hardly touching computers learned to navigate computer programs that let them talk with students and keep records on whether students had checked in and were working on assignments. The pace of change was dizzying.

As I write this book, in the summer of 2020, schools around the country are grappling with whether and how to reopen school buildings in the fall. Even those preparing to reopen are simultaneously trying to plan for another shutdown if health concerns require it. Faced with the massive need in Chicago, Jackson mustered a citywide effort between internet providers and Chicago philanthropies to guarantee high speed internet to one hundred thousand students for four years. She said she hoped it would provide a blueprint for other cities and jurisdictions to ensure that every student has a way to communicate with teachers.[56]

The district also stepped up efforts to get teachers trained on the new voluntary curriculum that had been being rolled out in a more leisurely fashion, so that what students need to learn was clearer to teachers, students, and parents.

At the same time, the district was facing what Jackson called "eye-popping" expenses related to opening buildings, estimating that it would take $75 million just to ensure the safety of students and staff members in terms of providing masks, shields, extra cleaning supplies, and thermometers. And that raises the difficult question of cleaning crews. In 2014, under Jackson's predecessor Forrest Claypool, CPS began turning over the cleaning of school buildings to private companies unaccountable to principals and local school councils. By 2018 newspapers were running stories about Chicago's filthy schools riddled with rodent problems.[57] In the spring of 2020 CPS announced plans to reestablish control of the building maintenance, but contracted with Aramark to provide cleaning services for one more year in order to give the district time to ramp up a new system.

This didn't exactly inspire confidence that the buildings could be made safe and sanitary for the fall of 2020. Whether because of that or because of general worry about COVID-19, many parents and teachers said they were wary of returning to school buildings in the fall.

Without new federal funding to reopen schools—which was still uncertain in August—CPS would have to make some "tough choices," Jackson said. "We're always making tough decisions in the education space in this country and that is really unfortunate."[58] On August 7, she announced that school would begin remotely, at least initially.

The other difficult conversation that Jackson led in the summer of 2020 had to do with policing, specifically policing in Chicago schools. As a principal in two high schools on the west side of Chicago—areas riven with violence during the years she was there—she had relied on police officers assigned to the schools, known as school resource officers. But, she said, in the wake of the conversations following the murder of George Floyd, "My views are evolving."

High school local school councils decide whether to have a school resource officer, and without a major restructuring of governance that would not change. However, Jackson said, CPS had been reviewing discipline policies. A review of the data had revealed that some policies were being used as catchalls to suspend or expel African American males disproportionately. A change in them had caused a 67 percent reduction in suspensions over two years. That was not good enough, though, and she said she would continue to look at discipline policies. "We can't dismantle 400 years with one policy," she said, but "it is the job of schools to disrupt the school-to-prison pipeline."

This conversation was not an abstract one for her. In May she posted an open letter to CPS families: "Today, I'm writing to you as a mother of a black boy who is worried for him, and the millions of other black boys in our country. I worry that when he leaves our home to ride bikes with his friends, he will come back to me as a headline, a hashtag, a rallying cry—an Ahmaud, a Breonna, a George."[59]

Heading into 2021, Chicago Public Schools is perched precariously in a city—in a country—whose economy could be devastated by COVID-19 or bounce back better than ever; a nation whose commitment to democracy could be destroyed or reconfirmed.

It could continue its march toward improvement or be set back significantly. As Sharkey said back in 2017, "We are really in danger of sabotaging something which is worthy of some celebration."[60]

This uncertainty means that the story about Chicago has a bit of a ragged feel to it.

But the point I want to make here is that over the course of the last three decades, Chicago Public Schools improved. It has improved more than any other large district in the country. Its improvement should be noticed and studied for the lessons it holds, not only for Chicago but for other districts around the country.

That is not to say that Chicago's exact path can be followed by other districts. Too many aspects are unique to Chicago, including the existence of its philanthropies and foundations, its universities, and its tradition of community organizing and activism.

But the fundamentals can and should be emulated and adapted to local contexts by school and other community leaders—a community-wide commitment to improving the lives of children by improving schools; a willingness to seek out facts in order to make better decisions; and an agreement that the job of school districts is to help principals organize their schools in ways that help kids get smarter.

CHAPTER 3

"Systems Elevate Averages"

The Story of Steubenville, Ohio

When the *New York Times* published Sean Reardon's first scatter-plot of over twelve thousand school districts in 2017, one of the more dramatic outliers was a little dot sitting pretty much by itself far to the left—meaning it is high poverty—and above the average achievement of the country for third through eighth grades. That little dot was Steubenville, Ohio. When I asked Reardon about it, he said that actually, at third and fourth grade, Steubenville was toward the top of the country. It slipped somewhat from fourth to eighth grade, which is why the first chart showed it as just above average, but its third and fourth grades were competitive with some of the wealthiest districts in the country.[1] (See figure 3.1.)

I was happy to see that, because I have been going to Steubenville since 2008, when I was drawn there by the top-of-the-state performance by one of its elementary schools, Wells Elementary.[2]

Over the years I have tried to puzzle through why Steubenville is so successful, and I have kind of settled on the phrase "programs plus culture." But that is too simple. So let me try and convey what some of the complexities are.

One story that sticks in my mind is from when I went to speak to the former superintendent, Richard Ranallo, a few years ago.

Ranallo had retired a few years before, and when I arrived at the designated middle school conference room late in the afternoon, I was

FIGURE 3.1

Socioeconomic status and grade 3 achievement

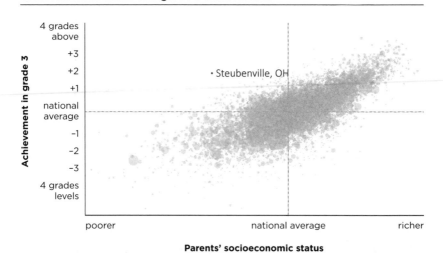

Source: Figure is based on SEDA 3.0 data (https://edopportunity.org). © sean f. reardon

surprised when many of the administrators in the district trickled in. Principals, assistant principals, district office staff, even a few teachers. Many of them had been hired or trained by Ranallo; they missed him and they wanted to hear from him as much as I did. It wasn't a big room so we packed in, some people standing along the sides or sitting on tables.

In his gravelly voice, Ranallo told us about how his father had grown up in Steubenville, whose factories and steel mills had attracted white workers from elsewhere in Appalachia and Black workers from farther South, as well as immigrants from Ireland, Italy, Greece, and Eastern Europe. Ranallo's father followed his own father into the mill, and when Ranallo was young his family lived "on an alley" downtown, within walking distance to the mill on the Ohio River that divides Steubenville from West Virginia. Finally, his family saved enough money to move up the hill, away from the dance halls and bars.

Ranallo graduated from high school, went off to Kent State University, and returned to teach in Steubenville in 1971, eventually becoming principal of Steubenville High School.

Everyone in that room was younger than Ranallo, but he was speaking to their experience. They all had a father or grandfather who had worked in the mill. You could hear a pin drop when Ranallo said that one day, after he had become high school principal, he went into the steel vault that stored generations' worth of records to look up the 5" x 7" card that held his father's permanent student record. His voice cracked as he relayed the judgment that some anonymous teacher or administrator had written about his father: "Poor student. Not much chance."

On that day in 2013, with most of the factories and mills shut down, Steubenville was one of the poorest cities in Ohio. The rusting steel mill hugged the river; downtown buildings sat empty and crumbling; thousands of people had moved away in the previous decades. The educators in that room knew that many people outside Steubenville were perfectly willing to write off them and their students in just the same way Ranallo's father had been dismissed in 1935. Back then, Ranallo's father was able to get a job at the mill. "He provided for us," Ranallo said. "We had a good life." But that possibility no longer exists for most Steubenville students. Steubenville's educators told me repeatedly that they feel it is up to them to "change the path of poverty."[3]

Changing the path of poverty is hard to do in a chronically underfunded district. But with a combination of thriftiness, canny grantsmanship, and Ohio's school choice policy, Steubenville manages to offer preK to every four-year-old in Steubenville as well as all-day kindergarten and college classes to their high school students.

The reason Ohio's choice policy is important is that state and federal funding follows any student who attends school in another district. For the most part, suburban Ohio districts refuse to accept students from cities, and most city districts don't bring in many students from the suburbs. But Steubenville attracts about eight hundred students every year from outside the city limit—almost a third of its twenty-five hundred students. Steubenville City Schools uses the money those students bring for onetime uses, such as renovating the high school, and to pay for college professors to teach their high school students.

Part of the reason Steubenville attracts so many students from outside the city limits is that the town has a strong hold on its former residents. Even if a Steubenville family moves out of town, they will often send their children back to Steubenville for school. As one high school student told me, "When you have a parent that went to Steubenville, their kids are guaranteed to go to Steubenville. You're not going to send your kids to any other school. That's how it is in this area. It's a pride thing." Added his friend: "We kind of hold ourselves to a higher standard than other schools in the county and surrounding area."

It's hard to convey the deep sense of community exuded by Steubenville, but I have felt it every time I have been there. "The majority of the people who work here, there's just this sense of community, a familiarity, tradition," said one longtime Steubenville resident, teacher, and parent of Steubenville students. "I have a bag full of winter coats someone dropped off this morning," said another, saying that the person ran across a clearance sale and thought the school's children could use them. "The church groups and everyone collaborate with the school to provide to those less fortunate in the community. It is a big calling in this town."

A newcomer told me that she was startled when she first came to Steubenville. She would ask her standard question to try to bond with children: "What's your favorite sports team?" Instead of what she expected—the Steelers or the Browns—children from preK to high school would say, "Big Red," meaning Steubenville High School's football team. "That was something that I was taken aback by. But I'm like wow—I mean they are really proud to be a part of Big Red."

There aren't a lot of newcomers though. Most people who live and work in Steubenville City Schools are themselves from Steubenville. "We always say it sucks you back in," says Steubenville High School graduate and fifth-grade teacher M. J. Burkett. "It's like a family. We grew up together."

Burkett, who is the local teacher union president, said that even the union-management relationship is one of familiarity. "We haven't filed a grievance in years," he said, because "we have these candid conversations and are able to work things out." In his regional meetings with union officials in other districts he hears what he calls horror stories that would never happen in Steubenville. He gave as an example that the union contract requires teachers to tell the district by July 15 if they are not returning to work in the fall. If a teacher misses the deadline, he tells the teachers that they can be held to the contract, and that other districts would do so. But, he said, "The superintendent says 'I don't want them here if they don't want to be. If their heart's not in it, they're not going to be effective with the students.'"

When the union contract came up for renewal in the spring of 2020 in the middle of the pandemic, negotiations took only a couple of hours.

That, of course, is enormously different from Chicago, which had a major strike in 2019.

But over the years I have seen in Steubenville other things that mirror what I saw in Chicago, namely an understanding of the importance of school leaders and systems to help educators go through endless cycles of data collection, monitoring, analysis, review, and adjustment in order to continually improve the success of their students.

Of course, the way those things play out are completely different from Chicago, but so is Steubenville's context. It has one tiny Franciscan college, not three major research universities and dozens of other higher education institutions. It has a Rotary Club and a small public-school foundation, not the Chicago Community Trust and dozens of other foundations. It has a drooping downtown and tiny tax base, not skyscrapers and the Chicago Stock Exchange.

But funnily enough, longtime school board member and Steubenville native William Hendricks told me that Steubenville was once known as Little Chicago. That nickname had nothing to do with schools and a lot to do with Al Capone. "Prostitution was prevalent here, gambling." Every neighborhood grocery kept a book of numbers, and cigar stores doubled as bookie joints, Hendricks said. "Nobody thought anything of it," he said. "I didn't realize how terrible it was until I visited some of my relatives away from here."

That was back when Steubenville was thriving—the mills and factories were in full swing and, as Hendricks said, people had money in their pockets. At a certain point organized crime in Steubenville got cleaned up. There's probably a story there, but the even bigger story is that money and people drained out of the city as industry shut down in 1980s and 1990s. When Hendricks's childhood friends come back to visit, he said, "They are devastated," and ask, "What happened to Steubenville?"

Many cities that have suffered such economic losses have seen their schools become mired in low performance. But in Steubenville, just about every third and fourth grader meets state reading and math standards and just about all students graduate from high school, half of them with at least some college credit.[4]

ESTABLISHING EXPECTATIONS

Steubenville City Schools wasn't always so high performing. It was accustomed to outperforming its neighboring districts and, Ranallo said, was known for being "very progressive." Its high school, built in the 1940s, had been the first million-dollar school building in the state and was known for its college preparatory program. Steubenville had full-day kindergarten and a preK program for children with developmental delays.

All that led to a certain level of complacency punctured in 2001, when Ohio legislators passed a law that said that fourth graders would have to meet state reading standards before moving on to fifth grade.[5] At that point only about two-thirds of Steubenville's fourth graders were meeting state reading standards.[6]

Melinda Young, who is currently superintendent but was then the brand-new principal of Wells Elementary, remembers asking teachers, "Who should fail?" *Her* answer was no one. But unless the elementary schools did something radical, some of Steubenville's students would be held back.

Ranallo was then assistant superintendent in charge of federal grants, including federal Title I money. The federal government at that point was urging Title I schools to adopt Comprehensive School Reform (CSR) programs, meaning programs that used what the feds called "scientifically based research and effective practices" to improve whole schools rather than the more piecemeal approaches that many Title I programs had been using. CSR had started in 1998 and was later incorporated into the 2001 No Child Left Behind version of the Elementary and Secondary Education Act.[7]

Ranallo urged teachers to study the research and select something that would ensure that all students learned to read. Longtime teacher Dianne Casuccio happened to see a story on the news about a high-poverty Texas school that had improved with a program called Success for All and was intrigued enough to learn more.

Success for All (SFA) was developed in the 1980s for Baltimore City Public Schools by two researchers, Robert Slavin and Nancy Madden, both professors at Johns Hopkins University. The idea was to incorporate all the extant research on how children learned to read and do math. From the beginning SFA included explicit phonics instruction, tutoring, frequent assessment, teacher read-alouds, careful data monitoring, and cooperative learning, meaning that students talk together and work together on projects. Even though the Baltimore schools using SFA outperformed demographically matched controls, a new superintendent swept it out of the city in the 1990s. But by then it had spread to other schools around the country, mostly with high concentrations of children from low-income backgrounds. In 1999 a group of education organizations had published a study, *An Educator's Guide to School Reform*, that reviewed the research on twenty-four comprehensive school reform programs. Although many were found to have promise, only three were found to have strong evidence of positive results: Direct Instruction, High Schools that Work, and Success for All.[8]

Ranallo liked that SFA provided a full curriculum from preK through eighth grade as well as training and support.

"But now the problem was," he said, "how do we change from each school doing their own thing?"

He and Casuccio were able to convince the superintendent and the district's principals, but "then we had to sell the staff." To avoid a situation where a principal or superintendent thrusts the program on an unwilling staff—a sure prescription for disaster—Success for All requires that 80 percent of teachers vote in a secret ballot to adopt it. Ranallo and Casuccio laid out the research, and when they convinced Steubenville's elementary teachers to try it, applied for a $200,000 federal grant to buy materials and training and to pay facilitators in each of the elementary schools.

For the most part individual schools, not whole districts, adopt SFA. But Steubenville was acting on what has become its mantra: Systems Elevate Averages.

"Even if you have a better way, being consistent is the better way," is the way current superintendent Young puts it. This commitment to consistent systems applies to everything the district does, from discipline

policies to computer programs. Among other things, consistency provides constancy for students and families who move among schools. But
in talking about Success for All, Young said, "Having a stable program,
curriculum, whatever you want to call it going from preK through eight
really makes a difference." In this she was echoing Ranallo, who put it
this way: "If you have a system that goes grade level to grade level, it's
less adjustment for the learner and you see better results in that."

Although both are fans of SFA, neither thinks that it is the only path
to success. "There are so many good programs," Ranallo said. SFA has
provided the framework for building coherence and marshaling the full
power of the district. But choosing the program was just the beginning.

"People have to buy into the vision. And if they don't buy into the vision, they don't do it. It's not going to work," Ranallo said.

The first year the schools implemented only the reading curriculum.
Teachers like Lynnett Gorman, who today is principal of West Elementary, found it helpful. "As a new teacher it was pretty easy. It was scripted.
It was a relief to have the guidelines to follow," she said. "I think the
seasoned veterans had a difficult time adjusting to the format of Success
for All's scripted lessons. They thought at that time it was a loss of the
freedom to just teach whatever they wanted to teach in the way they
want to teach it."

SFA provides scripts for every lesson and expects teachers to teach
every component of the program. This has led to a lot of resistance
among teachers around the country, but the Steubenville teachers I
spoke with said that they were willing to give up some autonomy for the
success of the students. And, they would add, they could still bring their
creativity to *how* to teach even if not *what* to teach. "We would encourage a new teacher to follow the scripted lesson," longtime teacher and
SFA coach Edie Boyde said. "The second, third year, that is where they
begin to tweak it to make it work for their students and for themselves.
So, it's not as scripted as the way people perceive it to be."

One hallmark of SFA is that students are grouped for reading and
math instruction according to their skill level, which is assessed every
eight weeks. This means that children are getting reading instruction
at their level the entire reading block. Traditionally teachers would use
the reading block to teach three different groups sequentially, while

the kids not immediately being taught would write out spelling words or do some other seat work. Simply regrouping kids to their level allowed them to get ninety minutes of reading instruction a day instead of thirty.

All the professionals in the building are conscripted as reading teachers, and the most highly skilled teachers are assigned to the students who are working on the most foundational skills. The idea is always to accelerate the students in the lower groups as fast as possible, but if children need help on sound-letter correspondence, then that is what they work on during reading instruction; if they have mastered that, they work on more advanced skills. To make sure that students can join the appropriate reading group, all students have reading and math at the same time. SFA has frequent formative assessments and protocols for how teachers collect data, display it, and analyze it in collaborative meetings dedicated to puzzling through the problems that students may be having.

In other words, Success for All is a complex program. It requires extensive data collection; it requires teachers to work together to study the data to individualize instruction; it requires that school leaders be part of all professional development so that everyone understands the research base of the program; and it requires that schools involve families. And over the years it has changed in light of new research and the experience of schools, which means teachers and principals need to continually learn new things and collaboratively solve the inevitable problems that crop up.

Still, despite its complexity, that first year went relatively smoothly. The second year Steubenville added the math curriculum, and teachers found the program overwhelming and wanted to stop. "There was storming," is how Young described it.

"Our principals knew they were going to go through some of these stages of change," said Ranallo, who by this time had become superintendent. "So, our leaders were able to hold [the teachers'] hands and talk them through." Ranallo distributed copies of a book written for businesses that argued that most businesses don't fail because they don't have a good plan but because they don't persist long enough to make the plan work. The schools hobbled through that second year.

"Once we got that system in, we could see we were making progress. The trouble was getting the system in," Ranallo remembered in 2017.

At this point, two decades later, it is hard to find a teacher or principal in Steubenville who doesn't champion SFA as a big driver of its success. But even within the universe of schools that have adopted SFA, Steubenville is a standout, which means that Steubenville's success can't be attributed simply to a program. SFA's cofounder Madden attributes it to leadership. "It's had thoughtful leadership and has for twenty years, which is really unusual."

Simply sticking to the program for so long is one reason for Steubenville's success, she said. She has often seen new superintendents bring a "different vision," sweeping out SFA to bring in another program, paying no attention to evidence of effectiveness of either one. "We often get booted. And it's never based on whether the schools are successful," Madden said. "The chaos of districts is so destructive. If there were respect for the evidence in what is important in student achievement, it would be an amazing steadying factor in education."

Echoing the research from the UChicago Consortium on School Research, Madden said, "Schools have to work as a team to create the condition where every student succeeds. The individual teacher can't do it alone." The point of Success for All, she said, is that it provides a system to bring "the school together as a team."

DATA FOR DECISION MAKING

When Steubenville's educators looked closely at their achievement data, they could see that there was a marked difference between the performance of children who had been in Steubenville's preschools and those who hadn't. "We give them a good start," says preschool teacher Melisa Karas. "And I think that's why . . . we're successful. I think the kids who go through our program, when they get older, it's helping them definitely to be better learners and nicer community people."

Data on language development, ability to play with other children, learn to read and write—they all backed up Karas's belief. So did the observations of the kindergarten teachers. "I can tell from day one which students came through our Curiosity Corner [preschool] program into

Kinder Corner and the ones who did not come through," said kindergarten teacher Michelle Moss.

Acting on that data, over the years Steubenville has added preschool classrooms until, in 2018, it offered preschool to every single four-year-old in Steubenville. When I asked Superintendent Young how she paid for twelve classes worth of preschool, she said the Ohio Department of Education gave Steubenville a $260,000 grant, she uses some Title 1 money, and the rest is from general funds. "It's an expense that pays dividends over and over again." She added, "I don't think preschool costs us a dime because we get so much back." She attributes the success to the high quality and good training of the city's preschool teachers who understand child development and language development.

But looking closely at the data also pointed to the fact that Steubenville's achievement after fourth grade needed to improve. "We have to get better. We look at results and try to evaluate the results," is the way high school principal Teddy Gorman put it.

For a long time, Steubenville's educators had worked on the assumption that as students achieved at higher levels at the elementary schools, achievement would naturally improve at the middle school—which in Steubenville begins in fifth grade. But that hadn't happened. The middle school was like many middle schools in the country, where individual teachers worked separately and with little collaboration. And student achievement hadn't really budged.

In 2017, I sat with the district's leadership team—which included Young, other district staff, and the principals—and I told them about Sean Reardon's finding that the third and fourth grades were toward the top of the country but that after that they fell in terms of their national standing. I was curious what their reaction would be. They all nodded. No excuses, no explanations. They had known that was the case from their data before Reardon's analysis. They simply nodded agreement and then said things like, "Not for long," and "We've got a plan."

After a great deal of deliberation, district leaders had agreed to extend Success for All to the middle school and hoped to see improvement. And by 2019, most grades had improved a lot. For example, in 2016 only 24 percent of eighth graders had met state English Language Arts standards; by 2019, 64 percent had.[9] Math and science had similar gains.

Switching wasn't easy, though. The middle school teachers weren't used to the kind of collaboration and prescriptive instruction that SFA requires. "Everyone teaches reading now," M. J. Burkett, the fifth-grade math and technology teacher, told me. "It was difficult at first," he said. As he learned the program and gained confidence, though, he said, "Reading is now one of my favorite classes to teach."

What SFA brought to the middle school was what it had brought to the elementary schools—not only a reading curriculum, but a structure of assessments, data gathering, and collaboration that would have been difficult to create from scratch.

But even Young—who is as strong a booster of SFA as you can find—will say that Steubenville's success "is not about a program."

She says, rather, it is about the clear vision that all students can achieve and a continual cycle of problem solving by school and district leaders to help them do so. "Always having that belief that we can move these students and that all students can learn."

MAKING BETTER DECISIONS

In 2013 Steubenville faced a crisis that tested the city's resilience. After two high school football players were arrested and charged with raping a young woman from a neighboring town, a blogger accused Steubenville of having a "rape culture." The blogger, who had lived in Steubenville for a while some years before, called the city "Rapeville" and accused the city as a whole of encouraging athletes to think of themselves as unaccountable princelings who had seigneurial rights over female students. Her descriptions of the incident, pieced together from Tweets and You-Tube videos posted by others at the parties attended by the young people, were lurid and gained national attention. The evidence was always murky and difficult to sort out but that didn't stop hundreds of activists wearing the Guy Fawkes–style masks of "Anonymous" from descending on the courthouse holding signs like, "Rape is not a sport!" and "The World is Watching!"

The local prosecutor had charged the young men as adults, but the judge who came in from Cincinnati decided to try them as juveniles, which normally means the proceedings would be closed to the public.

However, the same judge also decided to televise the trial, which meant that the identity of the young woman and the two young men became public, and the story was all over network news. The young men were found involved—the juvenile court version of guilty—on the basis of evidence provided by three other high school students who had been granted immunity from prosecution by then–Ohio Attorney General Mike DeWine, who is currently serving as governor. The convicted young men were sentenced to and served a year in juvenile detention.[10]

A grand jury later indicted six adults in the school system with either not reporting child abuse or concealing evidence. The technology director of the school system pleaded guilty to erasing files from the superintendent's computer. Then-superintendent Michael McVey maintained that he had followed proper record-keeping procedures but resigned just before his trial was about to begin; DeWine said his resignation satisfied the needs of justice and dropped the indictments against him.

When all this happened, I found myself wondering if the school system I had seen as committed to helping students succeed was really some kind of—I don't know how to put this exactly, but—sort of a bizarre cesspool of evil. Was the close-knit community that I had seen really a massive conspiracy to conceal deep secrets more troubling than those held by any other community? That's how Steubenville was being described.

In a rather remarkable statement in November of 2013, DeWine alluded to this portrayal and countered it:

> The message from the grand jury is this: This community is rectifying the problems. They are fixing things. They are holding people accountable. Several investigators, who played a prominent role in this case, live here in Jefferson County. The grand jury, itself, is comprised of citizens of Jefferson County. No one knows more about this case than this grand jury. They heard the evidence. They heard the witnesses. People made bad choices, and the grand jury said there are repercussions. There are consequences. And, there has to be accountability. This community has suffered so much. I personally feel for the citizens and what they have endured. And, I know that they desperately need to be able to put this matter behind them. What we must take away from these incidents is this: All of us—no matter where we

live—owe it to each other to be better neighbors, classmates, friends, parents, and citizens. We must treat rape and sexual assault as the serious crime of violence that it is. And when it is investigated, everyone has an obligation to help find the truth—not hide the truth, not tamper with the truth, not obstruct the truth, and not destroy the truth.

I have always known this to be a great community—a resilient community. And though our investigation uncovered some very bad things, it has also reaffirmed some very good things about this community—about the people, about the kids, and about their determination to move forward.

It's time to let Steubenville to move on.[11]

Moving on was, of course, easier said than done.

Among other things, the incident had inflamed regional resentments against Steubenville that have long existed. It's hard not to believe that some of that hostility comes because Steubenville has a substantial African American population and its schools have been integrated since before *Brown v. Board of Education*, while much of the surrounding area maintained segregation long after 1954. As one student said to me, naming a nearby school district, "Everybody thinks that Steubenville's a bunch of thugs. You can ask Indian Creek parents—they think Steubenville's a bunch of dirty kids and hoodlums. For some reason they always think that, but this is the cleanest school around here." Or, as a longtime teacher said, "We have our haters."

After McVey resigned, Richard Ranallo came out of retirement in 2014 to serve as superintendent one more time.

"Steubenville had this cloud over it," he said. "Steubenville didn't do something terrible. Steubenville got labeled as doing something terrible because a couple of kids did a terrible thing at the time." But, he added, "When there is a cloud over you . . . you start to internalize and think, well maybe I'm not doing something right."

The high school brought in a community program to help students talk through what had happened and to help them make better decisions than the students involved in the incident had made.

Ranallo told me that the board's instructions to him were to keep focused on the main thing: educating kids. He took the district back to his original playbook—find an innovative program with good research behind it and then provide the leadership necessary to make it work. But this time they were focused on the high school. "We wanted to get our kids to start thinking, 'We have value,'" Ranallo said.

They ended up focusing on two programs, the first of which was College Plus, which is a statewide effort to encourage high school students to complete college credits before graduation.[12] Steubenville had long worked with the local community college to help a small number of students earn associate's degrees by the time they graduated. They were mostly students who had previously been identified as gifted. Steubenville High School expanded that program to any student interested and able to pass the college's Accuplacer entrance test. "Sometimes a kid's not identified as gifted but they're pretty darn sharp and they can take that test and pass," high school principal Teddy Gorman said. "I'm not here to hold them back." Gorman said they are "shooting for the moon" and hoping that half of the graduating class would earn an associate's degree by the time they graduated.

In addition, Steubenville adopted High Schools that Work, a comprehensive school reform program developed by the Southern Regional Education Board (SREB) in the 1980s.[13] Gene Bottoms, SREB's vice president, who helped form the program, said its creation was spurred by the widespread elimination of vocational programs in the 1980s after the 1983 *Nation at Risk* report had lambasted vocational programs as being academic wastelands.[14]

High Schools that Work is a full-school effort, requiring that high school faculty attend trainings and conferences, principals reschedule their classes and leadership structures, and that everyone agrees to engage in a problem-solving cycle that is, in essence, the scientific method—from identifying a problem and doing a root-cause analysis to monitoring the results of solutions and adjusting in the light of evidence. Like Success for All, it provides a structure and systems for faculty to collaborate and move a school forward.

In addition, it has developed curricula and materials for nine programs that high schools can choose that work together with college preparatory courses as well as college classes to prepare students for careers. "We're very big on every student ought to have a focus in school.

Something in depth," Bottoms told me. "Some kids will have a fine arts focus—band, choir, music will be a focus for them. If you get everybody with a focus they begin to see the connections between the academics and their applications. When they have a goal in mind, they know where they're going, and they have an adult mentor all the way through high school who stays with them, you will greatly increase the percent of students going on to further study, and you'll reduce your discipline problems dramatically. You'll change the nature of teaching and learning."

Steubenville initially chose two of the career programs: Aviation and Aerospace Engineering and Innovative Science and Technology. It later added Health Informatics and Global Logistics and Supply Chain Management. "We follow a system where you start from the beginning and then you get to the finale," said Natalie Campana, who heads up the Aviation and Aerospace Engineering program. "And that finale will build a bridge for you to go onward to a four-year school, a technical school, or, if the job market allows it, you can go and work in the career field. That's what our goal is."

So, for example, in her program, "Year one we have aviation; year two aviation and airport management; year three meteorology; year four aviation pilot training; and we have the aerospace engineering also combined," she said. "It's giving students an opportunity—a taste—of multiple different careers and then they can gain a skill set using their academics and blending it with aviation and aerospace engineering." Steubenville High School has paired with the nearby Jefferson County Airpark as well as Pittsburgh International Airport, twenty-five miles away, to provide students with real-life experiences. Through grants they secured a flight simulator to begin training students to fly airplanes, and have developed relationships with Jet Blue and American Airlines.

"It's very advanced compared to other local schools down here," one aviation student said about Steubenville High School, adding that a nearby school was still using the same books and materials his father had used when he went to school.

While high school principal Gorman says that College Plus and High Schools that Work are helpful, he cautions, "I don't think that necessarily programs are the key to achieving more. I think you win with people. It's making sure that the right people are in those right programs."

Campana is one of those people, and she clearly brings tremendous passion to the job. A fourth-generation Steubenville resident, Campana's great-grandfather came to the United States from Italy because his education was cut short by World War I. He worked in the mill—and his sons and grandsons did as well—but he was determined that his family would be educated, she said. "There are seven teachers in the Campana lineup who have that passion for educating and helping others succeed. It's a valley tradition."

Like many other teachers in Steubenville, she sees the schools as the way forward for her students and her town. "We're very proud of our home, our culture, our school," she said. "And, yes, we might be in the rust bucket but don't judge us for that because we're still educating and inspiring and motivating our students for a better future."

And when I asked a random high school student to describe his experience at Steubenville, he seemed to echo Young's words: "Anybody in this school—any teacher, any faculty or staff—they do anything to help the student and anything to better the community."

Through the years the person who has been my guide through Steubenville has been Melinda Young, who I first met as principal of Wells Elementary and then as the federal programs coordinator and finally as superintendent. In many ways she embodies the culture of the district. She seems to know everyone and keeps an eye on all the details, but trusts the school and other district leaders to do their jobs. "With our leadership meetings, nobody in that group is more important than somebody else. We're all the same, we're all equal," she said.

"My leadership is giving individuals—and people responsible for particular programs—the freedom to do what they think is best, using data," she said. "In the back of my mind is the question, 'Is it good for kids? Is it the right thing to do for kids?' And that's how I base my leadership. But it's giving them the freedom to be their own leaders as well."

She and her team have to make tough decisions on what they will spend money on, and one thing they do is make sure that every grant that they apply for is aimed at their larger goals of improving student engagement and academic achievement. "Everything we do we do because we believe it has some kind of effect and helps keep kids in school and keeps kids engaged," she said. "I don't have a band program because

I think it's nice to hear the band during a football game," she said. "We have band because it's good for kids: It's good for kids to be part of a team. It's good for kids to learn a musical instrument. And it makes them want to come to school."

Over the years, she said, "We've done programs that haven't worked or we've done programs that we miss the mark—but they were done with the intention of making things better for kids—making a better learning environment and giving students something that they need."

CHAPTER 4

Exposing and Learning from Expertise

The Story of Cottonwood and Lane, Oklahoma

I first visited Cottonwood, Oklahoma, back in 2009 because the elementary school, the only school in the district, was performing at the top of the state. I was impressed by its approach to—well, everything, really—but especially its approach to reading instruction.

To my disappointment, Sean Reardon's first analyses in 2016 didn't include tiny districts like Cottonwood.[1] But when I called to check in with Cottonwood's superintendent, John Daniel, he suggested I look at Lane, about twenty-five miles away. I might never have noticed it without Daniel's suggestion, but according to Reardon's analysis it "grew" students as much as Chicago did.[2]

That set me off on a data journey.[3] (See figure 4.1.)

Traveling through the data, I could see that not only did students at Lane improve through the grades—as Reardon's analysis indicated—but the district had improved through the years so that, among other things, third graders were doing better in the years since Reardon's 2016 analysis. Lane still wasn't where Cottonwood was, but it had improved a lot, which intrigued me.

The story Daniel told intrigued me even more.

Some years before, he had gotten a call from Lane's superintendent, Roland Smith. Cottonwood and Lane had fairly similar demographics,

79

FIGURE 4.1

Socioeconomic status and grade 3–8 achievement growth

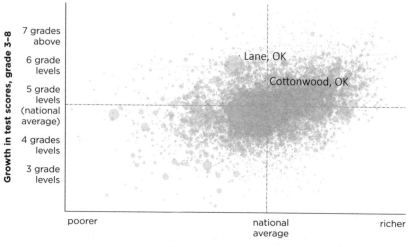

Source: Figure is based on SEDA 3.0 data (https://edopportunity.org). © sean f. reardon

but Cottonwood was much higher performing on state assessments. Daniel invited him to visit and showed him what was going on in the preK rooms, the kindergarten classes, and on through the grades. Smith's reaction was one of surprise. "He said, 'I've been doing it wrong,'" Daniel told me. After that, Smith sent teams of teachers to learn from Cottonwood's teachers, and that was the beginning of Lane's improvement.

In this chapter I'll explore what the teachers learned and what they did with that information. But first I want to point out that an educator whose district was not educating children as well as it should looked for a higher performing district and asked the most powerful question that exists in the field of education: "Your kids are doing better than mine—what are you doing?" The answers he heard convinced him to change his work, and his district has been improving ever since. This is the kind of thing every educator in the country could do. But I want to note that such a process requires two things:

- A common set of publicly reported data. It doesn't have to be test scores, though that is what I use for this book and what Roland Smith used to find Cottonwood. It could be suspensions and expulsions. It could be graduation rates. It could be teacher retention or parental satisfaction. There are a lot of measures of school success, and all can be used to expose expertise. But it needs to be commonly defined and it needs to be public, because that way everyone understands and can use the data.
- Educators willing to look at data with a professional eye, divorced from their personal predilections and prejudices.

The second part is hard, and requires some real toughmindedness. After all, people do what they do because they think it's the right thing. To have that challenged can feel very threatening. "We leave our egos at the door," is the way Sharon Holcomb said Lane's educators deal with that.

Holcomb has been at Lane since before Roland Smith arrived as superintendent in 2003 and remains after he retired in 2017. Smith told me that he'd like to take credit for what happened at Lane, but "all I can take credit for is listening to Sharon." Her official titles are curriculum director and director of special education, but she is also the grants manager, professional development director, and the district's liaison to the state department of education, among other things. She grew up near Lane, attended Lane as a child, and has worked there for thirty years. She is Lane's institutional memory, and was my guide to the school, inviting me to visit and showing me around.

She says Lane has always been known to be committed to its students. But back when Roland Smith became superintendent in 2003, it was not known for high achievement.

In fact, it was rather widely known for what Roland Smith calls "turmoil." Smith's wife, knowing he wanted to be a superintendent, suggested he apply when she heard that Lane was searching for its fourth superintendent that year. A longtime high school teacher turned principal, he had never encountered anything like Lane. "I was green. I didn't know anything about anything. I certainly didn't know all the problems they had."

Like Cottonwood, Lane is a small district with one school that goes from preK to eighth grade. Even though its district covers 200 square miles, it only had 137 students at that time.[4] About 80 percent of Lane's students come from low-income homes and about 40 percent from Native American homes, mostly Choctaw. Located ten miles outside of Atoka in southeastern Oklahoma, Lane is about as rural as you get—with the possible exception of Cottonwood, twenty-five miles away. Its original small one-story building has been supplemented by several additions of large, well-equipped classrooms connected with walkways and ramps, giving a maze-like feel to the campus. But that is the result of years of renovations and additions led by Smith, who walked onto a campus with a dirt parking lot, a 1976-vintage school bus, and cafeteria freezers filled with rotting chicken. "If I ever wrote a book about district leadership, I would say the first thing a superintendent should do is check to make sure the electricity is on," Smith said.

Smith spent several years trying to clean up and renovate the campus, the budget, and staffing before he called John Daniel at Cottonwood. He had been hearing about Cottonwood's success and he didn't believe what he had heard.

"I'll tell you what happened. John Daniel is a good, decent man, and I'm very coarse. We didn't talk about weather, football, fishing, anything. I said, 'John, this is what I think. You've been number one in testing. Here's what I think—I think your teachers are cooking that test. Show me different.' He did not get mad at me. He didn't raise his voice at me. He said, 'Let's go for a walk.'"

Daniel is used to his fellow superintendents thinking that Cottonwood is cheating. His response is always to invite them to see Cottonwood. But those who visit don't always understand what they are seeing. "They roll their eyes a lot," is how Cottonwood's librarian, Susan Eddings, puts it.

Smith, however, took it all in. "My epiphany was to understand—from John Daniels—the importance of reading," he said. "He's like a little pearl hidden away in Cottonwood, but he could teach early childhood at the University of Oklahoma."

What did Smith see at Cottonwood? He saw a school where the teachers understand what it takes to ensure that every student learns how to read. They know that it takes being able to hear the sounds of the language, map the sounds onto the letters, and how to decode quickly enough that you don't forget the beginning of the sentence by the time you get to the end of it. It takes knowing enough vocabulary and background knowledge that you don't get stopped too often by words and concepts that are unfamiliar, and it takes having some strategies to be able to think about what you're reading so that you comprehend it. Learning to read takes a lot of effort and a lot of instruction, at least for most people. At Cottonwood, three- and four-year-olds begin by playing rhyming and letter-matching games and dancing to sounds. By the time they finish the first quarter of kindergarten, they are reading. By the time they are in second grade they are writing fictional and nonfictional treatments of the same topics.

"The ones that we can start and go through the system and let them get that broad base—they don't struggle," says Cottonwood's Daniel about students who start as three-year-olds.

"That frees up our resources for those that do."

Students who struggle at Cottonwood are generally those who come in from other districts, often because they have failed to learn how to read in their home schools. Ninety percent of Cottonwood's students come from outside the tiny two-square-mile district, and many come in with a designation as having a learning disability. "We don't recruit," Daniel told me. But the state permits interdistrict choice, and families who hear about Cottonwood's success bring their children from next-door Coalgate or even from Ada, thirty miles away. Like at Lane, most meet the qualifications for free and reduced-price meals, and about 40 percent are Native American, mostly Choctaw.

When students arrive, they are quickly assessed and are "taken back to zero," as they say at Cottonwood, meaning the place where they are successful. If a sixth grader barely knows his letters, then that is where instruction starts.

"You would be amazed how quickly those skills pick up," says kindergarten teacher Doris Snow. "And you would also be amazed at how quickly their self-esteem picks up." Everyone at Cottonwood knows that when kids come in not knowing how to read, they are likely to feel shame at being a failure. They are also liable to be discipline problems. "Because they can't function academically," Daniel said. "If you get the academics taken care of and they can function, then when they get in high school they can stay on task because they're not trying to keep from doing something they can't do."

Cottonwood has long taken in students—and the state and federal funding that followed them—who have failed in other districts. But there was a time when students continued to fail after coming to Cottonwood. That was back before 2000, when Teri Brecheen became superintendent.

Like Smith, Brecheen is now retired, but her story is worth telling because she led the initial improvement that Daniel has since built upon.

SETTING A VISION AND DEVELOPING EXPERTISE

Brecheen's first job as a teacher fresh out of Southeastern Oklahoma State University was in now-closed Olney Elementary, not far from Cottonwood. In her class that year was fourth-grade John Daniel, the same one who is now superintendent. The class had had substitute teachers for the previous four months. "We were bored out of our minds," Daniel remembered. The students had spent a lot of time reenacting television shows, including the complicated drama about slavery in America, *Roots*.

"Fourteen boys and two girls," Brecheen said, who were "all over the place—reading wasn't good, math wasn't good." The only test available to her was a Stanford Achievement Test, and the average score was K.7, meaning that overall, the students were performing at a kindergarten level. "But they were a bright group of kids," Brecheen said.

For his part, Daniel says that the day Brecheen arrived in his fourth-grade class was the day he began to learn.

After teaching in Olney, Brecheen taught third and fourth grade in Cottonwood. "I saw the same situation in that class. Some kids couldn't read, some were way ahead." She and her husband, a cutting-horse trainer, then moved to Texas for his job, and she taught in a school serving the children of Spanish-speaking agricultural workers. "Same thing," she said about the students—some couldn't read, some were way ahead. When Brecheen and her husband returned to Oklahoma she taught first grade in Atoka, where for the first time she taught African American children.

"There was a belief system that if they were African American they wouldn't learn the way the other kids did," Brecheen said. Often the explanation had to do with the fact that many of the African American children came from low-income families. "I finally realized this has nothing to do with economics," she said. "They weren't being taught pre-reading skills," she said. "If we did it right, we could solve the economic issue." It was in Atoka, Brecheen said, where she really began understanding how to teach all children to read.

School board members in Cottonwood, hearing that she had returned from Texas, tried for three years to recruit her to be superintendent of their tiny little district. "I never wanted to be a superintendent or principal. The idea made me sick," she said. But Brecheen, a deeply religious woman, eventually felt that God was calling her. "I was furious. Why did He want me to do that?"

A new administrator preparation program had opened forty miles away, and she took seventy hours of credits in a year and a half to be able to take the job. With seventy-eight students, ten staff members, and abysmal test scores, Cottonwood was considered failing by the state. For her part, Brecheen didn't know how the teachers could manage to teach full classes of students when some were so far behind their grade level. "We had kids in eighth grade who were reading on a first-grade level—they felt ashamed, hurt, they felt like a failure." Teachers, she said, were "trying to meet all the needs, and there's no way to do that. To me that was a waste of those children's time."

She thought deeply about how to solve the problem. One day, she said, she heard God tell her, "Put them where they belong." She may also have been channeling her grandmother, who had been a one-room schoolhouse teacher. "I thought, how did they teach them then, and how did they teach them so much better?"

She began grouping students by skill level in reading and math, much as her grandmother had years before. Mornings at Cottonwood were two and a half hours of reading, writing, and spelling instruction followed by an hour of math instruction. In the afternoons, students would be in their home classes for science, social studies, and physical education. "Kids were rolling in and out of those classes, so no one knew where anyone belonged. We tried to make it safe."

Her essential goal was summed up as: "Nobody's going to get out of here without knowing how to read."

It should be noted that Brecheen had arrived in Cottonwood at a time of great upheaval in the world of reading instruction. Individual researchers like Sally and Bennett Shaywitz of Yale University and Jack Fletcher of the University of Houston were publishing important studies of dyslexia and learning disabilities. The *American Educator* published Louisa Moats's "Teaching Reading *Is* Rocket Science" in 1999.[5] The National Research Council had published *Preventing Reading Difficulties in Young Children* in 1998, and the National Reading Panel published its report in 2000.[6] All of that work pointed to the same thing: some children needed, and all children benefited from, systematic instruction in phonemic awareness, phonics, fluency, vocabulary, and comprehension strategies. And the standard practice of waiting until fourth grade to offer specialized help to students with difficulty reading was disastrous.

The National Reading Panel's report declared hopefully that its review of the research should end what had been known as the "reading wars." It didn't.

The report had challenged a powerful ideology of reading instruction called "whole language," and whole language proponents were not swayed. Whole language philosophy posits that learning to read is akin to learning to speak. Adherents argue that just as no one has to explicitly teach babies to speak, no one needs to explicitly teach children to read. Instead, children should be surrounded with written language and great stories.[7] Parents whose children weren't learning to read were urged to spend more time reading to their children and told that the worst thing to do would be to explicitly teach sounds and letters because it might kill children's interest in reading. Whole language swept through the nation's schools in the 1980s and 1990s and still holds great sway in teacher preparation programs.

At this point, researchers have spent decades studying every part of the whole language theory and have found little support for it. The human brain evolved to accommodate spoken language; we are indeed hardwired for oral language, which means that as long as babies' hearing is intact they don't need to be taught to speak. But writing systems are only about five thousand years old, and we've only expected most people to learn to read for a century or so. In order to read we have to repurpose parts of our brain that evolved to scan the horizon for predators and search the ground for berries. Although reading comes easily to some people, most children need explicit, systematic instruction in the mechanics of the written language. That doesn't mean they don't need to be entranced with great stories and surrounded by wonderful language. It also doesn't mean that learning the fundamentals has to be boring or tedious. But it does mean teaching children to divide words into their component parts of syllables and sounds and put them back together as words.[8] Otherwise, many children arrive in eighth grade, like those children in Cottonwood, mired in academic failure and shame.[9]

Brecheen, who developed a personal interest in this issue when she realized her son had dyslexia, read as much about reading instruction as she could find, and found Sally Shaywitz's work on dyslexia in children particularly powerful.[10]

Susan Eddings, Cottonwood's librarian and a lifelong friend of Brecheen's, told me that most of the teachers back then weren't particularly interested in changing what they were doing. But Brecheen had a way of encouraging teachers to try new things without making them defensive. "She would say, 'Let's try this for now.' And then she'd go and see if they were doing it."

Brecheen brought to Cottonwood the Voyager Universal Literacy System, a then-new program. Because it was so new, there was no research demonstrating its effectiveness, but it has since been found to possibly help with phonemic awareness, phonics, and letter knowledge.[11] Bringing in something new was stressful. "You don't know how to do it, you're trying something new, there's a risk. I thought the third-grade teacher was going to have a nervous breakdown," Brecheen said. She herself worried that if it didn't work, "I've shipwrecked a whole group of kids."

Voyager came with weekly tests, and Cottonwood teachers could see the progress that students were making. Not all students were successful with it, and over time Cottonwood brought in a whole battery of supplemental programs, many developed for students with learning disabilities, that they deployed with students who weren't making progress. At its core, though, Cottonwood's educators developed a clear idea of what students needed to know in order to learn to read, ways to measure whether they were making progress, and a commitment that no child would leave Cottonwood without being able to read. That meant that instead of committing to one way of doing things, they were committed to the success of kids and then tried different things that worked. "Seeing every child as a unique individual and giving each one their individual instruction is how all children can soar," Brecheen said.

They brought the same approach to math, and slowly Cottonwood—where, some years, 90 percent of students qualified for free and reduced-price meals—became one of the top-performing schools in Oklahoma.[12] As far as science instruction was concerned, Brecheen brought her memories of hating the way she had had to memorize science terms and repeat them on weekly tests. "The only thing I liked was the experiments." She wanted students to do nothing but experiments and then write about what they learned, and that's what she encouraged.

Meanwhile, John Daniel had become a scientist working for a company that provided field and lab analysis for the Environmental Protection Agency. He had tired of work travel and wasn't interested in getting the PhD that would allow him to advance. When his company asked for a five-year commitment, he quit and began working at Cottonwood as a science teacher and teacher's aide while he figured out his next step. "Mrs. Brecheen had been a spiritual mentor to me," he said about his decision to change fields. When one of Oklahoma's infamous tornadoes struck Cottonwood, tragically killing a fourth-grade teacher, Daniel finished out the year with the teacher's class while he took coursework to get his certification. "A lot of prayer went into that decision," he said. Brecheen began preparing him to take her place.

At a certain point they converted the gym to a huge science room for a science program that required computer stations where students worked in groups on hands-on science activities while being overseen by a teacher moving from group to group. It took a couple of years before the new gym—complete with a large tornado shelter—was built. Going without a gym for that long was a courageous move in sports-loving Oklahoma but, Brecheen said, it was important to do what was necessary to ensure children's learning.

Daniel gives Brecheen credit for building the foundation for the school's success. "She's the one that laid that foundation that every minute with a child is the most important." When I asked her why she had retired, she said she felt she had taken Cottonwood as far as she could, and that Daniel was ready to lead it to new heights.[13] When she left, Cottonwood had grown to almost 300 students and 51 staff members. Families whose children had failed to learn to read in their home schools were driving their children to Cottonwood from all over the area.

Under Daniel's leadership Cottonwood has remained toward the top of the state in terms of achievement, a feat made more remarkable by the fact that Oklahoma's legislature has been systematically starving its schools of resources. Cottonwood keeps going in part because Daniel is relatively successful in applying for grant money, and four of Cottonwood's teachers have retired and work for stipends. "That's a $15,000-a-year teacher you just talked to," he said, laughing, after I talked with one of Cottonwood's senior teachers. He wasn't sure how much longer that situation could last—sooner or later those teachers were bound to actually retire. He would have liked to hire some younger teachers to learn from the veterans, but his budget was too tight, and there is continual talk in Oklahoma of closing down what are called the "K–8 districts," rural districts that don't have a high school.

Educators in Lane, too, are worried about that and are hoping that its improvement will convince the state to let them be.[14]

LEARNING FROM EXPERTISE

One Lane teacher who welcomed Roland Smith's Cottonwood epiphany was kindergarten teacher Priscilla Jackson, who had been frustrated by what she thought of as his typical secondary attitude toward early education. "He thought we were babysitters," she said. Smith's visit to Cottonwood, Jackson said, "really turned a lot of things around."

When he returned from his initial trip, Smith realized there was a lot more to learn. "I told John, 'I will wear you out, I will bother you 'til you ask me to stop,' and he said, 'No, you will not.'" He called Daniel regularly to get advice and ideas. "He was always so giving and so helpful and so encouraging, and so uplifting," Smith said. "He could have kept his secrets to himself to lift himself up. There's just not many like him."

Smith also began sending teachers from the early grades to Cottonwood and later the older grades, as well. They found a welcome. "They were open to share ideas, to share resources, to say you're doing a good job. They weren't judging," said Holcomb. "Whenever I went with teachers that was what I saw—they were just, 'come with me and sit down right here and let me show you.'"

Cottonwood's systematic instruction in early reading—and the careful records they keep tracking which students have mastered which skills—came as a revelation to Lane's teachers. Beverly Marble, who is a special education resource teacher at Lane, says, "I had teachers just tell me, 'I wasn't trained in phonetics.' So then then they couldn't teach it."

Sharon Holcomb wrote a grant proposal to the state department of education, and all the teachers went for a week of training in Texas to learn the different skills involved in early reading. Even Marble, who had been taught some phonetics at Louisiana State University, found it revealing. "I didn't realize that reading could be broken down like this into all of the skills."

Today, resource teacher Marble and her colleague Ann Richardson keep careful records on every child third grade and below so that they know who has mastered the *oo* sound, who can complete simple rhymes, and who recognizes onset phonemes, among other things. The chart they keep covers a door, with each child a row and each skill a column. At the beginning of the year children are assessed, and yellow highlighter marks each skill a child is lacking. Classroom teachers teach these skills to their classes in whole groups, and if kids don't master a particular skill, the resource teachers, armed with the data for all the students, schedule them with a few other children who haven't mastered the same skill to work during "Eagle Time," a special time slot named for the school's mascot. The midyear assessments show a lot less yellow.

"In the medical field," says Holcomb, it's like "going to a specialist and actually having specific testing done [to] isolate exactly what's wrong."

What this means is that Lane students are getting both grade-level work and help filling in whatever gaps they have in small, specialized groups in a time set aside for all students to get extra help. All the adults in the building are part of tutoring during Eagle Time, including the school secretary and the librarian. Once they have mastered the early reading skills, students spend their Eagle Time on fluency, comprehension, and vocabulary, including prefixes, suffixes, homonyms, synonyms, and antonyms. Vocabulary is recognized as a schoolwide weakness and to address it, Lane has purchased a vocabulary program for the older children. But they're also beginning with the three- and four-year-olds by doing something that struck me as exceedingly clever.

Jessica Holder is a traveling speech therapist, shared by three different school districts. Twice a week she is in Lane and during that time works with a few individual children with severe speech needs, as most school speech therapists do. But her main job is to prevent children from needing individual speech therapy, and to do that she works with whole classes of three- and four-year-olds as well as kindergarten. She works with the lower grades on language development—vocabulary, sound recognition, pronunciation, and much more. She sets the agenda for the week, and teachers then follow through, working with their students on particular words, sounds, skills, and ideas.

"I've found that if we introduce these things to them when they're younger they're just like sponges, they just take it in and it's not a big deal," Holder says. "You might think, why would you do numerator and denominator with a three-year-old? Well, because if you tell them that's what it is, that's what it is. So when . . . they get to fifth grade, the vocabulary is not a problem."

When I mentioned to Daniel that Lane's speech therapist works with whole classes he immediately saw the value and said he would try it as well, a nice example of how ideas flow both ways.

Key to Lane's improvement, Holcomb told me, is that Smith encouraged teachers to say that they needed to learn more. "He was supportive of that and said, 'Let's find what you need.'" He didn't "make teachers feel guilty," she said, that they weren't already expert reading teachers. And he created schedules that gave teachers the time they needed to visit each other's classrooms and Cottonwood and to meet together to work through what they had seen and how they could incorporate new ideas into their practice. "Not to replicate the program per se exactly," said Holcomb. "But to make it work for our district and our kids with our teachers."

Smith, reflecting back on his years as superintendent, said there were three things that he thought were key.

- "You have to check your ego at the door and admit there are some things you don't know."
- "Second thing, as a superintendent you have to have some kind of knack for human capital—even out in Lane, in rural areas, there may be people who are coarse, but if you see their delivery skills or their pedagogy skills or their assessment skills or grant writing skills, you've got to be able to harness those skills."
- "The last thing is accountability—holding people accountable, even the teacher who has been there twenty years or thirty years, and letting them know we're all on the same team."

One key practice Smith instituted was to end school at noon on Fridays for students so that teachers could have a solid three hours a week to collaborate. They would discuss individual students and their progress or lack thereof and develop plans for how to address the issues involved, whether it was hiring an aide, changing a practice, or buying a piece of software. "When you do that week after week, month after month, year after year, you start seeing success," Smith said. "But it's long and arduous."

After years of effort, the state's superintendent called Smith to say that Lane had finally earned an A on the state's accountability scorecard. "I was bawling," Smith said. He called the whole school together, shook hands with every staff member, and played "True Colors" by Cyndi Lauper. "You've got to understand—our kids live in abject poverty."

Soon, other superintendents who thought he was "cooking the books" called him, just as he had called Daniel years before. He and Daniel would sit with other superintendents from southeastern Oklahoma and try to explain what went into being a successful school. "You could pour the testosterone like buttermilk it was so thick," Smith said about those meetings. "John Daniel would say, 'If Roland can do this, anyone can do it—if they are willing to do the heavy lifting.'" But, Smith added, the others too often wanted "instant pudding" and weren't willing to do the work.

When Smith retired, Lane's teachers were nervous that the new superintendent wouldn't continue the kind of culture that has allowed teachers to keep on learning. But the new superintendent, Pam Matthews—and the principal she brought with her from nearby Antlers, Ashley Willis—have brought the same approach to ongoing improvement. "The best thing you can do is say, 'I don't know but I'm willing to learn and I'm willing to find it out,'" says Matthews. "There's nothing wrong with not knowing. What's wrong is if you don't find out and learn."

That attitude, Holcomb says, is important for students as well. "If the students see the teachers working to improve and admitting that we made a mistake but we're going to try to correct that and learn, then they understand it's okay to make a mistake and that learning is a lifelong process."

Like Cottonwood, Lane has been starved of resources. Like Daniel, Holcomb is in a constant search for grant money. Many of the grants she has been able to get have been for technology, so Lane's classrooms are equipped with white boards, Chrome books, and other gadgets. Right before I visited she was able to secure a grant to build classroom libraries of books, a fact that made the teachers I talked with almost giddy with excitement. They would finally have enough books to feed their students' insatiable appetite for reading. "We shouldn't have to put this much effort into getting what we need to teach the future generations," Holcomb said.

Both Cottonwood and Lane have been able to take advantage of the education resources of the Choctaw Nation of Oklahoma, which among other things offers a six-week summer school to any child from kindergarten through third grade who is reading at the 40th percentile or lower on a national standardized test. The Choctaw Nation of Oklahoma spends millions of dollars a year in an attempt to "close the gap between research and best practices and rural Oklahoma" in the words of Todd Hughes, who heads up many of the Choctaw Nation's education efforts. The teachers who teach summer school share what is working and what isn't on closed Facebook groups that act as area-wide professional learning communities, and those communities are solidified at an annual summer conference that typically draws one thousand teachers and one hundred and fifty administrators to hear national experts talk about reading and other research. "That's very rare in southeastern Oklahoma," said Hughes. "Professional development costs money." The Choctaw Nation also provides analyses of school data that allows principals and superintendents to easily compare how their students are doing in comparison with other students in southeastern Oklahoma.

There is a lot more to say about Cottonwood and Lane—both are calm places where students are treated with respect, urged to ask questions, and encouraged to read a great deal. When I asked random students I ran across whether they liked to read, they could name favorite authors and favorite book series. When I asked them what they thought about their school they would say things like, "I learn a lot more here than my old school." Like Cottonwood, Lane takes in students who have been badly served by other districts. One parent told me that her son, who has epilepsy, had been bullied by teachers in his old school and not taught to read. She happily drives the miles to bring him to Lane where, she says, he is thriving.

And that is what keeps Holcomb in the job: "Seeing kids that have been thrown out and discarded and seeing them improve—seeing them come from other schools just beat down and seeing them succeed here."

But the point that seems important to me is that educators in both districts are on a continual search for better ways to do things to provide more opportunities for their students. And they have been willing to do the hard work to improve instruction for every single student, all of whom live in one of the most isolated areas in the country.

In fact, when the coronavirus forced the closure of school buildings in Oklahoma, it quickly became evident how few of the students were able to communicate with their teachers. Not only did many students not have Wi-Fi, many didn't even have cell phone coverage where they lived.

John Daniel took heart that the pandemic, having revealed deep inequities of opportunities, would spur the nation to address them. "Neat things could come out of this," he said.

CHAPTER 5

"A Strong Belief in Equity"

The Story of Seaford, Delaware

Delaware, Joe Biden has said, "has a shameful past, as related to race. A shameful past."[1]

In Southern Delaware, Seaford educators have confronted that past by committing to the idea that every child should be successful. "Our slogan is 'Success for All,'" said former superintendent David Perrington. "But it's not just a slogan. It's a belief."

Before I go any further I should tell you why I am talking about Seaford, Delaware, because the truth is that I don't really pay much attention to what most superintendents say. I would not be impressed with what Perrington had *said* if I hadn't known what he *did*. And the reason I know what he did was because I paid attention to a bunch of numbers on a page.

Those numbers began with one of the many analyses Sean Reardon has done with his gigantic database. He found a set of districts where African American students are gaining ground faster than white students. So, for example, while white students might on average grow by one academic year in a calendar year, Black students might grow 1.2 academic years. When I went through the list, many of the districts were too low performing for me to think they had a lot to teach others yet. Maybe in the future.

Seaford, with about thirty-five hundred students, stood out. Back in 2014, Seaford was performing way below the state. All groups of students were performing below their peers in the state, and Black students in particular were doing horrendously. By 2018 and then again in 2019 Seaford was performing at about the level of the state. But the younger grades—particularly grades three and four—were way outperforming the state. All groups of students in Seaford were improving, but Black students, students with disabilities, and students learning English as a second language were improving fastest.

This is exactly what we should want to see in any school or district— all groups improving but the groups that start out behind improving faster. In 2019 Black students in third and fourth grade had caught up to where white students in Seaford had been in 2014—the gap between them would have closed, except white students had improved at the same time.[2] (See figure 5.1.)

All of this made me want to know what was happening in Seaford.

At the same time, Sharon Brittingham had been telling me something important was happening in Seaford. Brittingham was one of the first principals I wrote about, back in 2007.[3] She was the fierce leader of Frankford Elementary School in the Indian River School District, which isn't far from Seaford.[4] She had led Frankford from being one of the lowest performing schools in the state to one of the top performing schools in the state. After she retired as principal she became senior associate director of the Delaware Academy for School Leadership at the University of Delaware. That means she coaches principals all over the state. She had been telling me that good things were happening in her hometown of Seaford, and the numbers backed her up.

When I went to observe, I found a set of educators who have successfully tackled a whole variety of issues, from school culture to quality of instruction, with a deep underlying commitment to equity and continual improvement.

Pretty much everyone told me that Seaford had really needed to improve. In 2014 two of its four elementary schools were on Delaware's "priority plus" list, and a third was about to go on the list, which meant the schools were in the lowest five percent of Delaware's schools in terms of achievement. The one middle school and the one high school in the district weren't doing fabulously, but they had not been identified by the state as needing improvement.

FIGURE 5.1

Grade 3 English language arts

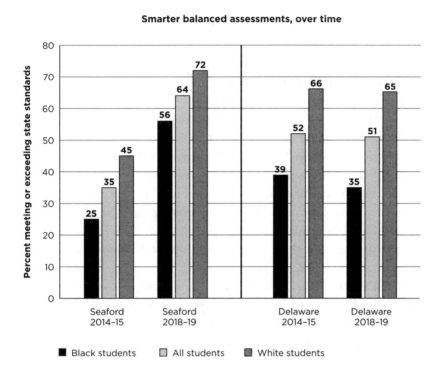

Smarter balanced assessments, over time

Source: Delaware state report card

That's when the school board hired Perrington as superintendent. He had been an assistant superintendent in nearby Caesar Rodney School District, and was nearing retirement. But he knew there were several openings in Seaford, and the lure of being able to build an administrative team was enough to bring him to Seaford for one last job.

"I knew this would be an opportunity for the right individuals if we could get the right team here," he said. "We could be extremely successful and our students would be extremely successful."

He and his team focused the lion's share of their efforts on the elementary schools initially, and that's what I will focus on as well. My hope is that over time we will be able to see the effects of the improvements in the elementary schools on the middle and high schools.

In any case, when Perrington arrived in Seaford School District—which consists of sixty-four square miles of mostly farmland framing the Nanticoke River, on which the towns of Seaford and Blades sit—he realized that he hadn't understood how dramatically Seaford had changed.

During World War II, the town of Seaford was known as the Nylon Capital of the World because of its DuPont plant. After the war, the factory switched to manufacturing Dacron, but DuPont remained the center of Seaford's economy. "Your parents either worked at DuPont or they didn't work at DuPont," Brittingham told me about when she went to school in Seaford in the 1950s and 1960s. "The teachers would ask on the first day of school, 'Raise your hand if your parents work at DuPont.'" Reared by her tenant-farmer grandparents, Brittingham was never part of the DuPont-country-club set, but back then every high school student knew there was a job waiting for them down at the plant if they wanted it.

The DuPont plant dwindled in the 1970s and 1980s with continual layoffs until a very stripped-down version was finally sold to Koch Industries. The jobs of well-paid line workers and even better-paid engineers, managers, researchers, and chemists were gone, along with much of the tax base.

Low-wage poultry jobs now dominate the area, attracting immigrants from Central America and the Caribbean, particularly Haiti. Today, Seaford has twice the level of poverty as the rest of Delaware and a very diverse population which includes not only the new immigrants but white and African American residents, many of whose families date back many decades.

NOT DEMOGRAPHICS BUT LEADERSHIP

"Seaford is not what Seaford was" is a more or less constant refrain, even today. And demographic changes were often the reason given for the fact that three of its elementary schools were failing.

Perrington brought a different lens to the issue. When he looked at the district, he told me, he saw inconsistent leadership—he was the fourth superintendent in four years, for example—and a district that had counted on programs fixing things. Seaford had bought lots of programs in the past few years. "We were program rich and instructionally poor," Perrington said. "These programs were the newest shiny item that was out there. It appeared to me that there wasn't a lot of critical analysis of the programming before it was implemented."

Rather than look to programs, Perrington counted on school and district leadership as the key to district improvement.

This didn't mean he thought teachers were unimportant. "It always comes down to the teacher-student relationships," he said. "It always is going to come back to that." But knew from his days as a school principal that the relationships he had built with teachers were key to whether teachers improved their instruction. And when he worked in the human relations office in his previous district, he found that teachers stayed or left their jobs primarily because of their principals. "The principal had a huge impact."

To fill leadership openings, he was looking for people with experience, though he didn't necessarily expect them to have experience transforming a low performing school or district. "I myself really had not been exposed to this type of challenge before." But, he said, he was looking for people who said, "I want to get better and I can get better at what it is that I'm doing." That quality, plus "perseverance and efficacy—I believe I can have an impact and influence people—those are the three things that I always look for."

From his former district he brought Corey Miklus, who had been an award-winning principal, as assistant superintendent for curriculum and instruction. He hired three elementary school principals that first year, and a fourth in his second year. By the time he retired in January 2020, he had hired all but two administrators in the district.

Everyone he brought in faced challenges.

Krissy Jennette, for example, began as principal of Blades Elementary in the middle of August, shortly before teachers reported to work that first year Perrington was there. When she looked at the data she saw that a very high 24 percent of fourth- and fifth-grade students—most of them African American and English language learners—had been identified as needing special education services. As she spoke to teachers, she found that they thought, "If I can qualify them as *something* then they're someone else's problem and I don't have to be responsible for their data." Jennette, who had been a principal in a high performing school in Maryland as well as a school coach for the Coalition for Essential Schools, let the teachers know that they would be held responsible for the progress all their students made. "And the teachers said, 'Well, if I'm going to be held accountable for them I don't want them going with someone else.' So, we started looking at shifting kind of our whole thinking and not doing as much pull-out service and doing more push-in services." Adjusting the way special education services were provided meant that Jennette had to redo the master schedules several times that first year as principal. But the work she put in meant that students were learning grade-level standards instead of being pulled out of fourth and fifth grade to do kindergarten math, as they had in the past.

Carol Leveillee, principal of Frederick Douglass Elementary School, also began by looking at data. "The year before I arrived there were over 350 suspensions," Leveillee said. Leveillee had been a highly successful principal in Maryland for seventeen years and was used to having to suspend maybe ten students a year, so 350 was a shocking number to her. She had taken the job because she had been impressed by the thorough interview process Perrington had put her through. She wanted a job near family, and, she says a little embarrassedly, she was charmed by Seaford's mascot, the Blue Jay. "Had I looked to see what I was getting myself into—as bad as it was, I probably would've said no. It was a toxic environment," she said. Many of the teachers and staff told her that they had had fourteen principals in twenty-five years and that they would outlast her.

Some of the teachers, Leveillee found, weren't prepared to teach. She gave as one example teachers who would give seven worksheets to kids who understood a math concept and one to those who struggled. "I would say, 'That's not what math is. That's not differentiation.'" Other teachers "would humiliate kids in front of whole classes for behavior," she said. "We had to really work on culture and how we treat people, how we treat kids, how we treat one another."

That first year she put a number of teachers on improvement plans. Some improved, some left. The support she got from the central office was key. "If it hadn't been for Duncan Smith that first year, I would have left," she said about the then–head of human relations. Perrington told me that, although he was never looking to get rid of people, he was "aggressive" about saying to teachers and administrators, "Your role is so important here that we can't afford to have someone who's not doing what they need to be doing for our students."

Leveillee got an insight into how her building had operated before she arrived when she remarked to a teacher that her hallway seemed darker than the others. The teacher pulled her aside conspiratorially and told her that the teachers on that hallway had asked the maintenance person to take out a lightbulb because they didn't want her looking closely at the bulletin boards where they posted student work. The previous principal had pulled down student work and thrown it on the floor because it was substandard. "I said wow, I really appreciate your sharing this with me," Leveillee said. She told the teacher to tell her colleagues, "'I just want some kids' work out here. Promise them I will not rip one piece of student work down.' I spent the next three months at faculty meetings highlighting something from that hallway."

That was part of her general campaign to celebrate any success, no matter how small, in order to build morale and a sense of efficacy. "I celebrated every little victory we had—if we had a kid win a coloring contest for fire prevention, the whole world knew about that. I mean, I could have cared less they were coloring. But you know what? We had positive press."

Meanwhile, the third principal Perrington had hired in those early days, Becky Neubert, was at Central Elementary School, the one elementary school in the district that was not considered by the state to be low performing. Neubert had been a principal and data coach and was attracted by Perrington's promise of leading improvement. "We were a good school in the district, but not across the state," she said of Central. Students were doing "okay," she said, making it clear that okay was not sufficient.

At that time, Central was the "choice" school in the district. Delaware law says that parents can choose to attend any school in the state that participates in the choice program if they can transport their children there. In the early 2000s Central had gone to a year-round schedule, which meant that instead of a long summer break there was a shorter break with intercessions during the school year. The original idea was designed for kids who struggled and for families who had difficulties managing child care during the summer. But over the years funding for the intercession classes had dried up and Central had become the choice school for savvy parents with the wherewithal to handle childcare in the off-kilter schedule. The school was economically and ethnically diverse, but it wasn't representative of the district as a whole. Perrington called the demographics "very skewed."

LEADING FOR EQUITY

The inequity of having schools with different demographics and vastly different levels of performance rankled. Perrington told Brittingham he "couldn't live with it," she told me.

After his first year as superintendent, he asked demographers from the University of Delaware to redraw school boundary lines so that they would evenly divide all the district's subgroups. To make the task easier he reorganized the elementary schools so that instead of having four elementary schools with kindergarten through fifth grade, there would be two K–2 schools feeding into two 3–5 schools.

Changing school boundaries is a dangerous enterprise for superintendents, who avoid it because it is so emotionally and politically charged. Families develop loyalties to school and teachers. When those loyalties are combined with hostility to children and families of different ethnicities and class backgrounds, the fights against boundary changes can be bitter, protracted, and career ending. Brittingham worried that Perrington would lose his job. "I didn't think he'd be able to pull it off, truthfully."

Perrington knew all that but persisted. "It was about equity," Perrington said. "Because to us, our feeling was these are community schools and these schools should reflect the community." He held several community meetings to explain the plan, which—importantly—was backed by the school board. Mike Kraft, president of the school board, said he told community members that "I'm going to hold Dave and his folks accountable" so that "you're going to love that school just as much as the other."

The principal who was perhaps under the most scrutiny from white parents was Leveillee at Frederick Douglass Elementary School, which was historically the African American school. Until the battle over school boundary lines, she hadn't realized that white families were zoned for Douglass but had "choiced" into Central. She had been too preoccupied with fixing what was wrong with Douglass to notice. But then she was inundated with worried white parents. "I spent my whole summer convincing parents that Frederick Douglass was an okay place for their kids to come."

Leveillee was able to assure them that Douglass was a calm and respectful school because by then she had made some headway on the school's culture. The restructuring of grades actually came as an unwelcome change to her because just as she had convinced the staff to start accepting her vision she lost half her staff and gained new third-, fourth-, and fifth-grade teachers. "I was really worried because we had made such progress," she said. But she had a "lot of courageous conversations," and "we didn't regress as much as I thought we would."

Over at Central, the other 3–5 grade school, "We took it as a 'bring it on,'" said assistant principal Chandra Phillips about the realignment. "The culture here is we're going to teach whoever you send us. It doesn't matter who you are, what you look like, what your background is, what your resources are. It's because we have teachers here who care about kids and have a passion for their job."

Today, all four elementary schools more or less match the demographics of the district: 33 percent white, 36 percent Black, and 23 percent Hispanic with 42 percent meeting the qualifications for free and reduced-price meals.

In addition, Perrington said, "We don't have this one stellar school out here where these other ones are low performing and not doing what they need to do. Now we've created a situation where all of our elementary schools have to work together and that seemed to work extremely well."

One unanticipated benefit of the reorganization of the schools was that teachers had more grade-level colleagues under one roof to share data, compare strategies, and learn from each other. That is, it was now physically easier for teachers to collaborate—but it still required a shift in culture among teachers who had been used to closing their doors and doing whatever they thought best.

BETTER INFORMATION
FOR BETTER DECISION MAKING

Perrington and his team of administrators agreed that the way forward was to share all the data and information about how they were doing among all the staff. But sharing data exposes vulnerabilities — "that sense of transparency where you've got to sometimes take a gut punch and swallow your pride," said Central principal Neubert. "Myself included."

This is perhaps at the heart of Seaford's improvement, and it wasn't an easy shift to make. "We had to get over the hurdle of even putting that information out there," assistant principal Phillips said, adding that teachers felt that having their colleagues see their data was intrusive and threatening. But, she added, the data had to be transparent in order to get to the place where a teacher whose students hadn't been as successful as another teacher's could say, "What are you doing in your class?"

This is all part of what Perrington calls applying "the scientific method," in which educators identify and research a problem, propose and implement a solution, and then monitor and study the data in order to see whether it worked. If it did, strengthen it; if it didn't, try another approach. He expected every teacher to do that with the problems they faced, such as ensuring that all children learn to read; he expected every principal to do that with the problems they faced, such as ensuring that all teachers have the time and information they need in order to ensure that all children learn to read.

To build the kind of team that could think and act in this way together, he took advantage of a Delaware State Department of Education offer to send the leadership team to training for low performing schools and districts at the University of Virginia Curry School of Education. It was there that the district and school leaders began to map out their first plans for how to improve and how to communicate to faculty, staff, and parents what they were doing. Instead of adopting a traditional five-year plan, they followed the recommendation of UVA's trainers and used shorter cycles of ninety-day improvement plans.

In their first ninety-day plan, they developed cycles and systems of intervention for students who failed to learn what was taught in their whole-group instruction (sometimes called Tier 1 instruction). In other words, when and how they would identify students to get additional help either in small groups or individually (sometimes called Tier 2 and Tier 3 instruction). Other plans included developing schoolwide behavioral systems, such as ways to walk in the hallways and behave at lunch, and building data systems so that teachers had the information they needed when they needed it.

"And then the constant cycle through that ninety-day plan was, you know, analyze, strategize, next. It's just this constant cycle of figuring out what works and what doesn't," Neubert said.

Each of the plans, Neubert said, was necessary and derived straight from information that teachers provided. And though each was ambitious, none was overwhelming. They "didn't take a lot of crazy effort that ruined our souls," Neubert said.

This constant cycle of problem solving, monitoring, and adjusting in light of data is what Perrington said would move the district forward. "I am talking about the scientific method—I'm just saying let's reintroduce something that we know works," he said. "In the other disciplines, it works—and it can work for us."

But bringing the scientific method to problem solving requires everyone involved to set aside their personal feelings, and that is where leadership comes in. "We don't have time—our sense of urgency is too high to be worried about egos," Neubert said. "We have to be willing to grow and fail together and share our failures—because we have plenty."

One of the failures they all had to confront was that far too many students weren't learning to read, and teachers tended to fault the students and their families. "It would be, oh my gosh these kids are coming in not ready to read and we're spending so much time to play catch up," said longtime teacher Tammy Steele. "There was a lot of blaming."

Thinking about what that meant for the district as a whole was the responsibility of the assistant superintendent of curriculum and instruction, Corey Miklus, who brought to his job a deep knowledge of reading instruction.

USING RESEARCH TO
IMPROVE READING INSTRUCTION

Originally trained in whole language reading methods, Miklus had begun teaching in Delaware in the 1990s.[5] There he was introduced to a more balanced literacy approach, which included some phonics instruction, though it wasn't explicit and systematic. As a result, he said, "I struggled as a teacher."

He began to understand the science of reading instruction when, as a principal, his school got a Reading First grant. "It blew my mind how much we learned. I was just so impressed." Reading First was a $2 billion federal reading program pushed for by President George W. Bush as part of the 2001 No Child Left Behind iteration of the Elementary and Secondary Education Act. Reading First provided money to schools and districts to use materials and training that incorporated the elements of reading instruction that had been identified by the National Reading Report in 1999 as supported by rigorous research. Those elements were phonemic awareness, phonics, fluency, vocabulary, and comprehension strategies.[6]

Miklus's school, he said, had been "a struggling school. But under Reading First you just kept seeing scores rise and rise and rise—and they became a Blue Ribbon school."[7] The key to success, Miklus said, was the training Reading First provided. "A lot of teachers become very dependent on the basal reader. Whatever the teacher edition says to do they do, but they don't know the background of why. I push for everyone to know the why."

When he came to Seaford he was faced with a dilemma. The year before, Seaford had spent half a million dollars on a new reading textbook series that, he knew, was neither aligned with Delaware's state standards nor with the science of reading instruction. The district's teachers had spent many hours adapting the series, rearranging lessons, and writing assessments. Knowing the history of school turnaround efforts, he was wary of telling teachers that they would have to change yet again. "In turnaround there is just no consistency—no consistency in programs, no consistency in teachers or administration," he said. "You might get lucky and a program lasts two years or the administration lasts two years and it just keeps cycling through."

He thought long and hard about how to navigate that situation without angering the teachers and spending a lot of money.

He consulted the person who had provided Reading First training in his old school and who had later been his doctoral advisor. Sharon Walpole, professor of education at the University of Delaware, told him that she was developing a new reading program. But rather than bring it in, they agreed to begin with training on what good reading instruction looked like. Walpole and her team began by training reading specialist Tammy Steele and the reading interventionists, many of whom were paraprofessionals.

"This was specific. If your child struggles with this, based on the data, you do this. It's very systematic, there's no time wasted," Miklus said. "The students were already struggling. You don't need to slow them down . . . They need more, they don't need less."

That spring Miklus and Walpole began providing the teachers with a few lessons with read-aloud books from Walpole's new program. "The teachers started liking the books, they started liking the questions, they had a little bit of a voice developing some things. So, we just kind of get bigger and bigger and bigger to the point we could say, 'All right let's go,'" Miklus said.

The following year, the district adopted Bookworms. Many teachers and principals in Seaford give Bookworms credit for the improvement in student achievement, which is ironic because even Miklus says, "We're about people, not programs."

Still, it's worth talking about Bookworms, because it has been associated with improvement not only in Seaford but in several other districts.

Walpole, together with her late partner, Mike McKenna of the University of Virginia, had spent years providing training for teachers in reading instruction and school leaders in how to provide time and support to teachers. "Then we think, well, it doesn't matter how much of that you do if your curriculum is bad," Walpole said. "So, we thought, what if we give that a go?"

They decided they would try to incorporate everything that research had determined was important in reading and writing instruction into a single package that regular teachers could implement. As a result, the routines of Bookworms are simple and repeated every day. Every day, students spend three forty-five minute chunks of time on reading and writing instruction, and every minute is prescribed. So, for example, at the beginning of the first forty-five minute chunk, students share with a partner what they wrote the previous day. The teacher then introduces a vocabulary word or two that they will need to know for that day's reading. They then read the day's grade-level text chorally, led by the teacher, for ten to twelve minutes—interrupted by a thirty second example of the teacher using a couple of words to illustrate how to visualize what is happening in the passage. Then students pair off and take turns reading aloud the same passage they just read for ten to twelve minutes, followed by a teacher-led discussion where students draw inferences from the text. It is all topped off with the teacher adding to a chart that documents what is going on in the book. These "anchor chart" documents allow students who are absent or a bit absentminded to be able to catch up with the story the next day when they repeat the process with the next chunk of text.

The point of having students reread what they have already read chorally, Walpole said, is that research has demonstrated that rereading helps build both fluency and comprehension. "That is one routine serving two masters," Walpole said.

Another forty-five minute chunk of time is divided up so that teachers meet with small groups of students who are working on different reading skills, such as phonemic awareness and phonics (for beginners) and morphology and spelling (for more advanced students). While the teacher is meeting with the small groups, the rest of the class is writing about the text they read in the first forty-five minute block and reading individually from books they choose. A third forty-five minute block is dominated by teacher read-alouds, where teachers read and discuss with students texts that are one, two, or even three grade levels above what students are able to read on their own.

All of it is scripted—the questions, the vocabulary, the book selections—everything, to make sure all the elements research says are important are addressed in the most efficient way possible so that students have more time to read.

"That was one commitment we made," Walpole said. "Another one was that all kids, regardless of the communities in which they live . . . should learn to read with the great stuff that our own privileged children had access to. So only real books, only good books, no excerpts." Book selections include many Caldecott and Newbery winners and lots of both fiction and nonfiction, including *The Watsons Go to Birmingham, 1963*; *Because of Winn-Dixie*; and *Harvesting Hope*, a biography of Cesar Chavez.[8]

The third commitment that Walpole and McKenna started with was that volume matters. "The more you read, the more incidental vocabulary growth you get," Walpole said. "Learning more vocabulary words and more content makes you smarter and gives you more choices later on." Over the course of kindergarten through fifth grade, children read or listen to 276 books and are encouraged to read other books they choose independently.

Miklus says that Seaford's growth can be attributed in large part to the systematic phonics instruction provided by Bookworms. But there are a lot of phonics programs out there. The thing that really attracted him, he said, was "the read-aloud component." The reason, he said, is that "students from poverty tend not to travel or they may not have the vocabulary in the home. If you have read-aloud books above their grade level, now they have experience with vocabulary and places that they can never get to."

Another thing that attracted him: the price. Bookworms is completely available online for free. The lessons, assessments, and routines are all available from Open Up Resources, as are training videos. Districts can pay for printed copies and in-person training, but the main cost of Bookworms is the trade books that form the core of the program, and they are much cheaper than any textbook series.

"The feedback was that the kids loved it—they loved the books, they didn't want to stop the reading. And when we heard that, we won," Miklus said.

Laura Amidon, who has taught in Seaford for nineteen years, agrees. "I love teaching through novels," she said. "I love the books, I love the incorporation of the writing."

Laura Schneider, principal of West Seaford Elementary agrees, with a slight proviso. "Providing scripted lessons, most of the time, is a good thing. I think sometimes the teachers feel a little bit stifled by it. But the routines that are common every lesson the kids really seem to enjoy. And the books are good books—it's real literature."

When I asked Walpole about her reaction to the idea that teachers might feel a bit stifled by the scripted lessons of Bookworms, she said, "Usually I say, 'Well, this isn't about you.' Kids actually love structure. Absolutely love it, crave it, it provides a safe space for them to learn—and the stuff itself is so interesting."

Nicole Somers, a longtime third-grade teacher, agreed. "I like that it's the same," she said. "We're following a plan, but we can still add our strategies." She said she found the routines such as the choral reading and the differentiation particularly helpful with her students who are learning English as a second language.

Longtime reading teacher Tammy Steele became such a fan of Bookworms that she now works with Walpole at the University of Delaware providing training for districts that adopt the program. "We've seen that it works with all kids, right? It works with all groups of kids from all different backgrounds," she said. "You see so many more kids just immersed in reading, carrying books with them to the buses, to the cafeteria, to the playground—you know, enjoying reading."

At the same time he brought Bookworms to Seaford, Miklus also put in a series of assessments that would gauge the learning of students at regular intervals. This allowed him to elide arguments about whether teachers needed to make their instruction more rigorous. "I knew it was going to be very hard for me to convince teachers that they had to up the rigor in the classroom," he said, anticipating that they would object that the students weren't capable of more rigorous work. But when teachers saw the assessments, he said, they would immediately start anticipating the difficulties their students might have and thinking about how to make sure their students learned what they would need to pass those assessments. "The greater purpose of wanting to see students be successful allowed everyone to dive in," he said.

It is those assessment results—along with other data, such as behavioral data and state assessments—that provide teachers the data they use in their professional learning communities to see who is succeeding, who not, and to then diagnose how to ensure that all students succeed. "The data gives us a starting spot to decide how we're going to help students," Miklus said. Because, he said, "at the end of the day there's a student behind the data."

Perrington agreed that opening up the data was key to Seaford's improvement, which he summed up as: "Understanding our population; establishing relationships; strong building leadership—and acceptance—beyond acceptance—a strong belief in equity," he said. "Equity's not a word that you use but it's in practice and you can demonstrate it every day."

One of the important things about Seaford's story, he said, is that it demonstrates that not only can "you be successful with diversity," but that "diversity adds to a school."

In the fall of 2019, Perrington announced that he would be retiring and moving to San Diego to be near family. I confess I held my breath until I heard that the school board had named Corey Miklus superintendent, signaling a continuity of leadership. The very first challenge he faced in January 2020 was to shepherd a referendum vote asking taxpayers to increase their taxes to pay for schools. "It's been years since the Seaford School District has been able to pass a referendum," he said. One reason it may have passed is that he was able to point to the enormous improvement in the elementary schools and plans for the secondary schools to build on that improvement.

But that was just the first challenge. Days after the referendum passed, Delaware closed its school buildings in the wake of the coronavirus pandemic, which meant that Miklus as a brand-new superintendent had to cope with what became an unprecedented interruption of schooling.

In the early weeks, Seaford schools handed out six hundred computers and worked with local companies to provide low-cost internet to families. But even though Delaware is small and, on the whole, wealthy, there are swaths of southern—or lower—Delaware where internet service is unavailable, and that includes Seaford School District's farmland communities. The district spent $8,000 mailing materials to students who live in internet-less areas and activated the food trucks that it uses during the summers to provide food to students to distribute thousands of meals.

Frederick Douglass Elementary principal Leveillee suggested that Seaford adopt an idea she had heard about years before in Chicago in which the whole community adopted a book. The district distributed thousands of copies of *The Boy Who Harnessed the Wind*, by William Kamkwamba and Bryan Mealer, the true story of a young boy in Malawi whose inventiveness and perseverance helped save his farming village from drought when he built a windmill that powered an irrigation system. Teachers and administrators read chapters for online videos in English and Spanish, and students were encouraged to build things from items found around their homes.

As the months went on, Sussex County, where Seaford is located, had thousands of cases of COVID-19 and hundreds of deaths, many of them centered on the poultry plants where many of Seaford's parents work. Miklus and the leadership team in Seaford spent countless hours on reopening plans without knowing if in fact school buildings would be able to reopen. Miklus worked with the state to establish internet to the more remote areas of his district so that if buildings couldn't open or couldn't stay open, students would still be able to connect to their teachers and schools.

"It's a challenging time," he said.

CHAPTER 6

"Everybody Can Rise Together"

The Story of Valley Stream 30, New York

When I asked Sean Reardon to name the district where African American elementary students do the absolute best in the country regardless of where they fall on the economic scale, he said, "Wyoming, Ohio." I spent a little time talking to folks in Wyoming, which is an interesting district right outside Cincinnati and, coincidentally, is Reardon's hometown. It's one of those towns where families move, as they say, "for the schools" but, because school taxes are high, often move away after their children leave high school. Mostly white with a small African American population, families and educators seem pretty serious about education and the district is extremely high performing. Although I was intrigued by some of the things Wyoming has been doing, it seemed so atypical that I wasn't sure it could serve as an example for other districts with more typical income levels.

So I asked Reardon for the second highest district in terms of performance by African American students.

And the answer came back: Valley Stream 30, where African American students performed 1.2 grade levels above the national average for all students in 2016. (See figure 6.1.)

Valley Stream 30 is one of three school districts in the village of Valley Stream, which is inside the Town of Hempstead in Nassau County, one of two counties on Long Island in New York.

If I just confused you by that description, it gets worse.

FIGURE 6.1

Socioeconomic status and grade 3–8 achievement, Black students

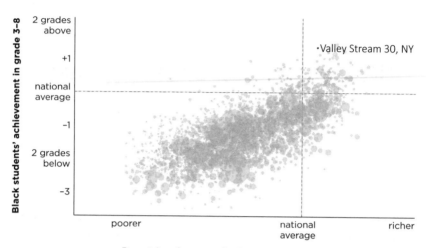

Source: Figure is based on SEDA 3.0 data (https://edopportunity.org). © sean f. reardon

With a population of 1.4 million people, Nassau County has two cities, three towns, sixty-four incorporated villages and more than one hundred unincorporated areas, all covered by fifty-six school districts, some of which overlap with other governance areas and many that do not. They don't make much sense unless you see the patchwork as, essentially, a way to maintain segregation.

Nassau County was home to the first major suburban developments built for returning World War II veterans. Thousands upon thousands of small single-family houses were built in the postwar period on what had been flat farmland, providing a release valve for crowded New York City. For the most part, African American and Hispanic families were prevented from buying those new houses by racially restrictive housing covenants and discriminatory housing loans. Today, decades after federal law made such housing discrimination illegal, Nassau County remains one of the most segregated places in the country.[1]

One reason is real estate agent steering; another, white flight.[2] When Black and Hispanic families move into the close-in suburbs, white families tend to move farther east on the Island. As a result, school districts near Queens that a generation ago were home to Italian Americans, Irish Americans, and Jewish Americans are now home to African Americans, Hispanic Americans, and Asian Americans.

That's the story of Valley Stream 30, an elementary school district that, along with two other districts, feeds into a combined Valley Stream High School. Just two decades ago, 40 percent of the roughly fifteen hundred students were white. Today, only about 5 percent of the students are white.

"When I first moved we were the first African American family on our block and now that's definitely the majority," parent Natalie Cange told me. The diversity of the district was what attracted the family of Sharon Japp Vandijk. "I am Indian and Chinese from Guyana," she told me. "My husband is Black-white-Spanish. He's Dutch, Black Trinidadian, and Venezuelan Spanish. We knew that the community was multiracial, multicultural. I looked at the breakdown of the school and we could fit in here."

Thirty-eight percent of the students in Valley Stream 30 are Black, 28 percent Hispanic, and 26 percent Asian, mostly the children of relatively new immigrants from India, Pakistan, and Bangladesh. About 45 percent of the students are considered economically disadvantaged. Although that is not a high concentration of low-income homes in comparison with a lot of districts around the country, it is a fairly high concentration for Nassau County.

In fact, its demographics and achievement attracted the attention of Josh Anisansel, a school administrator working in Farmingdale, farther east on Long Island. While working on his doctorate at Fordham University, Anisansel looked for a Nassau County district that has both a high concentration of poverty and high achievement for students from low-income homes. He identified Valley Stream 30 as meeting those criteria and became so convinced that it had lessons to share with the field that in the acknowledgments to his dissertation he wrote, "This is a story that should be shared!"[3]

What that means is that two different analyses—one that looked at the achievement of Black students in comparison to the rest of the country, and one that looked at the achievement of students from low-income homes in a Nassau County district with a relatively high density of low-income families—both identified Valley Stream 30 as an outlier.

Just to give a couple of data points, as of 2019, 67 percent of students in Valley Stream 30 met English Language Arts standards; in New York as a whole, 45 percent of students did. For those who would like to see proficiency rates in the 90 percents, so would the folks in Valley Stream. But the cut points for proficiency in New York are set at ambitious levels, so the comparison with the state as a whole is a meaningful way to look at the data. And it's even more meaningful when broken out by demographic groups. So, for example, 62 percent of students considered to be "economically disadvantaged" in Valley Stream 30 met state ELA standards, compared to 36 percent in the state. And 65 percent of Black students in Valley Stream 30 met standards compared to 35 percent of Black students in the state. To be even clearer, a higher percentage of Black students in Valley Stream 30 meet standards than white students in the state; a higher percentage of children considered to be economically disadvantaged in Valley Stream 30 meet standards than non–economically disadvantaged students in the state.[4]

All of which is to say that Valley Stream 30 has met the Ronald Edmonds test of having "outcomes you desire." When I went to figure out what they do to be more effective than other districts, I heard about high expectations for students and educators and a deep focus on systems of data and information to provide individual help for students and educators.

These are some of the same underlying principles at work in the other districts I profile in this book. But, of course, Valley Stream 30 has its own context and its own way of doing things.

HIGH EXPECTATIONS AND DIVERSITY

Here's how superintendent Nicholas Stirling describes Valley Stream 30. "It's a district that has high expectations and respect for the educational process. And It's a district that highly values diversity. Diversity is seen as a positive, not as a negative. It's celebrated and it's used as a guide to everything that we do."

Part of what Stirling means by that is that the diversity of the student body forces the educators to grapple with the fact that in order to meet the same standards, not everyone needs the same instruction. "When you really understand equity and respect equity and don't get caught up in [questions of] 'I'm losing out, or I'm not getting something,' you then start to see that everybody can rise together."

In many ways, this understanding of how diversity and equity work together are at the heart of the work Stirling and the other educators in his district do. "Whatever goals that you have set can be reached, but people will get there at different rates. And then you have to figure out how to accelerate some, how to maintain some, and how to make everyone feel as though they actually can reach those goals."

One of the things that struck me in Valley Stream 30 is that neither Stirling nor anyone else took the Reardon analysis all that seriously. They could have put out press releases about how high performing their African American students are in comparison to the rest of the country, and many districts would have done so. In Valley Stream 30 they are much more focused on the students who still are not meeting standards. "When you're at 60 or 70 percent, that's when serious work comes into play because you're now really focusing on moving the quarter of the student population that has the most need," Stirling said. "That's the work that we are in."

One of the many ways this plays itself out is that educators in Valley Stream 30 think deeply about the role background knowledge plays.

In previous chapters I talked about some of the things that go into early reading instruction—making sure children recognize the sounds of the English language, know how the sounds map onto the letters, and help them read quickly enough to not forget the beginning of the sentence by the end of it.[5] But that isn't all there is to reading. Another key is something that can be called word knowledge, which allows readers to understand what they are reading.

It may seem blazingly obvious that kids who know how to decode words and *also* know what those words mean will read better than kids who struggle to decode and don't recognize the words they're reading.

But this was something that actually required a great deal of research to establish.

The "fourth-grade slump" was first named by reading researcher Jeanne Chall in 1983 to describe a phenomenon that puzzled a lot of educators for many years. Kids would do reasonably well on third-grade reading assessments and then tank in fourth or fifth grade. A popular explanation was that kids lost motivation—a 2007 *Newsweek* article said they "lose their mojo."[6] Hormones, video games, all kinds of things were blamed for what seemed to be this sudden loss.

Careful research by Chall and others, though, established that students whose reading achievement dropped off often failed to have the academic vocabulary and background knowledge that was needed to understand the more complex texts they were expected to read beginning around third or fourth grade.

I remember visiting a Baltimore City school many years ago because I was puzzled about the school's achievement scores. The school, where just about all the students were African American from low-income homes, was beating the socks off of most of the state in third-grade reading but dropped precipitously in fourth and fifth grades. The assistant principal showed me around the school and I saw expert reading instruction that focused on early reading skills as well as comprehension strategies like asking students to find the main idea. I asked a few random kids to read to me, and they read picture books fluently and with expression, including one boy who read a folk tale set in China. Clearly the kids were learning to get words off the page. Afterward I asked the assistant principal what the school did to help the students understand the story—the geography of China, a little of its history, how Chinese names worked, and so forth. Her response was that the students didn't need it. You'd be surprised, she said, how much children learn from television.

That's when the fourth-grade slump became clear to me. Kids can get the words off the page and still not comprehend what they're reading if they have no background knowledge about what they're reading. Until third grade, students are generally reading texts that tend to require very general knowledge and use vocabulary that most kids know. But right around then they are expected to begin reading about history, geography, and science.

Obviously, part of the point of reading is to learn new stuff. But what adult readers sometimes forget is how much background knowledge is required before you can learn from what you're reading.

For example, a Maryland fourth-grade reading assessment question from a while back included a reading passage about Tad Lincoln's hijinks, like hanging a Confederate flag from the window and unleashing goats at a White House party, causing women to clutch their hoop skirts. Presumably the passage was chosen to appeal to children's sense of mischief, and they could learn something about Tad from that passage. But if they didn't understand the significance of the White House and the Confederate flag and why hanging it from the window in the middle of the Civil War might embarrass Tad's father, President Abraham Lincoln—or if they didn't know what goats and hoop skirts were, the whole passage would be a mystery and they would spend a lot of time puzzling through it. They might not be able to answer a lot of comprehension questions correctly.

The idea that you can rely on kids arriving in school knowing about Chinese geography or American history is preposterous. That's why we send kids to school—to learn stuff like that. Random television viewing habits are no substitute for a carefully built curriculum that systematically builds knowledge.

The fact that far too few educators understand the role of schools in building vocabulary and background knowledge has resulted in many schools and districts stripping their schools of instruction in history, geography, science, and the arts in order to spend more hours a day on reading instruction. The superintendent of my school district, for example, declared that all other instruction could wait in order for children to learn how to read. Because the district remained mired in whole language practices, this meant that not only did the district not provide explicit instruction in phonemic awareness, phonics, and fluency, the schools didn't even teach much content. Kids spent endless hours finding the main idea of random stories and predicting what would happen in a book from the pictures.[7] My kids' superintendent—and many like him—did not understand that, in the most basic possible way, history instruction is reading instruction; science instruction is reading instruction; field trips where students learn about the world around them are reading instruction.[8] All help build knowledge that permits students to be able to read.

Valley Stream 30 has a reasonably coherent curriculum and they teach history, science, and the arts and—at least until the pandemic hit—took students on a lot of field trips in and around New York City. But even so, educators are alert to the fact that they can't assume that their students will understand what teachers are talking about.

A science lesson that talks about marine life, for example, might assume that students understand what sand is and that sea water is salty and that tides push the water up and down the beach. But, Stirling said, "If a kid's never been to a beach, it's a very different type of lesson that you're going to have to provide."

The story that brought this home for educators in Valley Stream 30 comes from a few years ago when a teacher was teaching a unit on Jackie Robinson breaking baseball's color barrier. "The students were like, 'What is baseball?'" said principal John Singleton of Clear Stream Avenue Elementary School. "And the whole story gets lost if kids don't know what baseball is." Students who immigrated from the British Caribbean might have known about soccer; those from South Asia might have known about cricket. But baseball is a game that recent immigrants aren't always familiar with.

So, the school set about making sure their students knew about baseball.

Clear Stream faculty reached out to their local baseball team, the New York Mets, which sent over what Singleton called "a boatload of paraphernalia," including flags and hats. The gym was set up with bleachers and popcorn and halal hot dog stands, and they had a viewing of a baseball game, complete with explanations of the vocabulary—catcher, pitcher's mound, batter up, stealing bases.

"And then we went back to teaching about Jackie Robinson," Singleton said.

He added, "It's the same thing with any subject—if you don't understand the three types of matter, there's no way you're going to understand science. So you've got to give the background knowledge and the vocabulary for what matter is . . . and how things are liquids, solids, and gases."

Students arrive at school with widely varying vocabularies depending on the experiences they have had, the conversations they have had, and the books they have had read to them. "We know that for children of poverty and children of immigrants, building vocabulary is the number one thing to do," says Clear Stream's assistant principal, Yannie Chon. "So we have always embedded that in all instruction, in content areas as well as language arts."

Third-grade teacher Crystan Serra told me, "We have to front-load a lot of that background knowledge for our children. Some children don't necessarily come in knowing or having those experiences or exposure to certain topics. So we do a lot of work in that area to make sure that we're building their schema and we're building that background knowledge."

One of the systems Valley Stream 30 relies on to fill in knowledge gaps is RTI, or Response to Intervention. RTI was developed to move schools away from the traditional way they had provided students with extra help.[9] Traditionally, schools had used a combination of reading level and IQ scores. If students' IQs were, say, at average levels but their reading level was below average, that discrepancy would indicate that students had a learning disability and would be eligible for special education services.

There is so much wrong with the discrepancy model that it is hard to even know where to begin. But it held sway for decades, and probably lingers in some districts. In the late 1990s, the University of Houston researcher Jack Fletcher memorably declared that many children who had been identified as having learning disabilities suffered instead from "instructional disabilities" because they weren't being provided with effective reading instruction.[10] He and others demonstrated that the policy of what he called "waiting to fail" was disastrous for those children.[11]

RTI was developed to get students help when they need it, long before fourth grade. If students fail to grasp what is taught by the classroom teacher (referred to as Tier 1 instruction), as measured by some kind of assessment that is given and reviewed at regular intervals, they are provided small-group instruction (referred to as Tier 2 instruction). Those students who still need extra help are provided highly individualized instruction either in very small groups or one-on-one by a specialist.

Only after Tier 3 instruction is found to be inadequate is a student referred for screening for special education services.[12]

RTI is in wide use, and a major analysis has found it to have mixed results, depending on the school and district.[13]

But the folks in Valley Stream 30 say that RTI is core to their success. Michael DeBlasio is assistant principal at Forest Road Elementary and coordinates RTI for the district. He has worked in several school districts in and around New York City, and he says the way Valley Stream does RTI is what distinguishes the district. "We target students in need of support, research, and attach them to specific programs to support those needs. And then we have very rigorous monitoring of these students to make sure they are making growth. And if they're not making growth, [we ask] 'What are we doing to support these students in terms of trying different programs, trying different methods, trying different strategies to move these students?' That's something that was not happening in my other buildings."

Cathy Itri, a reading interventionist at Forest Road, agrees. "We have individualized interventions. In other words, it's not a one-program-fix-all."

If students need help in the early elements of reading—phonemic awareness, phonics, and fluency—they receive it. But just as importantly, they may also need help with knowledge.

"In fifth grade there's a lot of American history," said one of Valley Stream 30's eleven reading interventionists. "For a lot of students not born in this country, they don't have that background." She provides maps, photographs, and videos, and finds historic parallels that students might be familiar with from their home countries. "We fill in that gap in information so that they understand."

This kind of pre-teaching is particularly important for the 10 percent of students who are learning English.

"English language learners, in my opinion, are one of the groups that are less likely to participate in class." English as a New Language teacher Debra Iadevaio, said. Pre-teaching vocabulary allows them to "have this confidence instilled in them, and they're very proud when they raise their hands and are able to share with the class."

Kindergarten teacher Joyce Smithok described the overall process in this way: "We start off by identifying where the children come in, and it's almost like a one-room schoolhouse with a very big spread of ability levels. And then we target strategies, group children according to abilities, and we use resources that will help children in different ways."

She went on to say, "But I never want to talk too much about the science of it without saying that I think so much of our success is in relationships, in respect, in shared mission . . . My classroom has to be a safe, vibrant, nurturing community."

And that is another big part of Valley Stream 30 — the sense of community and the acknowledgement of relationships. "Education is a business about people, not about things," superintendent Stirling said. "Everything we do in terms of the foundation, we build upon relationships that we establish between students and other students, students and teachers, teachers and administrators, and teachers and families. Everything—everything—is built on the relationships."

Those relationships are centered on high expectations and treating everyone as an individual, but they are grounded in some very prosaic operating systems.

SYSTEMS FOR IMPROVEMENT

It is all very well to say that Valley Stream 30 has RTI. But what allows RTI to operate effectively is the master schedule. All the schools have an eight-period day, of which two periods are dedicated to what is called intervention and enrichment. "Those are the periods by which we really focus our efforts to enrich and intervene, where necessary, with our kids," Stirling said. "But at the same time, it's *only* during those two times that kids are pulled out."

The master schedule was one of the systems that most impressed Josh Anisansel when he was writing his dissertation. He has worked in a few different districts, and he has seen that students identified as needing help are often pulled out of classroom instruction, sometimes for multiple purposes, such as speech therapy, reading help, and math help. "What's so misguided about that practice is then the day becomes so fragmented—so the kids who need continuity *most* with their learning are the kids for whom we provide the *least* continuity."

By setting aside two periods a day for something other than whole-group classroom instruction, Valley Stream 30 has systematized the way students get individual attention. "If we believe in differentiation, it's not just providing less work for maybe the kids that are not doing as well," Stirling says, referring to the way many educators define differentiation.[14] "It's looking at how do you accelerate kids and how do you enrich the kids as well."

In many districts the only students who receive what is called enrichment are those who have been identified as gifted and talented by some kind of screening process. But in Valley Stream 30 all students are provided with enrichment. As part of that, students do a whole variety of activities from hands-on engineering projects to writing and performing plays and entering competitions such as spelling bees and the Jackie Robinson essay contest, a national contest that typically draws somewhere between ten and fifteen thousand entrants. In 2019, two fifth-grade students at Shaw Avenue Elementary were recognized by the contest—one as the national grand prize winner, earning the school a visit from Robinson's daughter.

"You don't necessarily have to meet a particular criterion—wherever you're at, how can you move to the next level and what can I do to support that? That's enrichment," Stirling said.

In order for teachers and principals to provide those opportunities for students, however, Stirling said that they themselves need opportunities to learn and grow.

"One of the things I'm most proud of is the type of professional development that is provided to our teachers on an ongoing basis," he said. "We have a comprehensive type of a system."

That system includes whole-district professional days, when teachers and staff members share their expertise with each other; Wednesday afternoon sessions, when teachers meet to learn about something related to school- and districtwide goals; Thursday afternoon sessions, when teachers meet to learn about something more individual to their own needs; opportunities to go to conferences or take online courses; and opportunities to visit other classrooms. And that doesn't even count the grade-level meetings, content-specific meetings, and Nassau County support office that offers in-classroom modeling of new computer programs or other technological assists. Twice a year the professional development committee comes together to look at the district's data and bring input from across the district about what professional development has accomplished and what more needs to happen.

"We talk about differentiation for our students," said Nicole Schimpf, director of special services. "What does differentiation look like for our teachers? You know not every teacher needs the same PD and they should not be sitting at the same time for the same PD. So we're really looking at having them provide that input to us and trying to create those unique pathways."

When I talked with teachers, they often mentioned the importance of professional development.

"When I worked in another school district I was denied going to some professional development because I was a newer teacher," said one. "I felt as though they weren't investing in me, whereas here right from day one they were investing in me. They were sending me to classes to get trained in certain programs. Any time I ask for any kind of professional development, they're willing to send me to get trained."

And just as RTI is supported by the much more prosaic master schedule, teacher professional development is supported by the more prosaic system of having contract substitute teachers who are on salary for a minimum of three days a week and invited to join professional development sessions. These are, generally speaking, certified teachers who would like to be hired as full-time teachers. This gives the substitute teachers a chance to know whether Valley Stream 30 is where they want to work, and gives the district a chance to see if they would like to hire them permanently when a teaching position opens up. In the meantime, they provide the cushion which allows teachers to visit their colleagues' classrooms, either within their own school, in another school in the district, or even in another district if there is something they think they can learn and bring back to Valley Stream 30.

All the professional development on building the expertise of teachers pays off when the district considers switching curricula. So, for example, when the data indicated that the math curriculum wasn't adequate, teachers throughout the district researched new curricula, piloted parts of it, observed colleagues piloting other parts, conferred, and agreed on a new curriculum in a few months.

"Honestly, that could take districts a couple of years to go through a new curriculum, do a curriculum audit, and then really implement a new one," said Christopher Colarossi, principal of Shaw Avenue Elementary. "We're talking about being done in a matter of months."

This kind of collaboration means that curricula are not imposed on teachers but rather provided as a resource. For years the lower grades used Journeys from Houghton Mifflin Harcourt as their ELA curriculum, and in 2018 the upper grades decided to adopt it as well. One of the reasons, principal Singleton said, was that Journeys "has everything." That is, it lays out the vocabulary ahead of time, it provides quizzes and tests and activities to go along with the lessons. "Let's not forget time is essential," he said. "So, since Journeys has it right there you can literally plan it out perfectly and use your time wisely."[15]

The collaborative curriculum adoption process is a way that the district makes a virtue of the fact that its size precludes having a large district office with specialized offices. Another way is that all the administrators take on districtwide responsibilities. So, for example, Clear Stream principal Singleton not only oversees Clear Stream Avenue Elementary, but also fifth grade, physical education, and social studies. "And it changes every two years," he said. "So that way everyone gets a different idea or different taste of all the different services that the district has."

This could be seen as making the administrators' jobs more difficult, but what I heard was that it allowed the administrators to learn and grow in ways that might in some ways be uncomfortable but that build their ability to lead. "Being a leader is being able to demonstrate to your colleagues, to your staff, that you're going to take a risk and that you're going to learn alongside them," Stirling told me. "And that's leadership."

This rotating list of responsibilities was part of how Stirling is building what he calls a "bench" of district leaders. He is quite clear that he is planning on retiring from this job. A career educator who began as a high school business teacher more than three decades ago, Stirling is openly working to build a leadership corps who can work across the district in a variety of ways and provide leadership in the future.

And so, when principal Colarossi arrived as assistant principal of Shaw Avenue Elementary, he was assigned to oversee first grade across the district as well as science, something that he initially felt relatively unprepared to do. "It was something I had to work on and build," Colarossi said. Within three years the district had secured a grant to improve its science instruction, instituted a "Skype-the-Scientist" program and a third-grade science fair, and opened a brand-new learning lab.

I was there the first day students were in the learning lab, and I thought Stirling would burst with pride. It was an old kindergarten classroom in a building that had long been shut to students. The room had been fitted with bright colors, new furniture, and a lot of technology for students to use—computers, drones, robots, virtual reality glasses, and more. Valley Stream 30's schools are all clean and well maintained, but they are tired and dated. Walking into the learning lab was like walking into the future. Third graders were working on their projects for the science fair and were talking about chemical reactions and layers of the earth. "You heard the level of language and their ability to talk with scientific terms," Stirling said. "That doesn't just happen overnight."

His point was that all the systems—all the schedules and professional development and building of relationships and routines and leadership could all be seen in that room where third graders worked together on demonstrations of basic scientific principles. "It just screams high expectations," he said.

But they also point to the fact that no one in the district works on their own. "The concept of closing your door and you doing it on your own is not something that will work in this district," Stirling said. "It's about sharing and being efficient in the work that you do. Time is not our friend. So we have got to figure out how to provide all this opportunity in such a very limited amount of time."

When the pandemic hit, Valley Stream 30, like all other districts, was thrown into a little bit of confusion, but it didn't last long. They spent two weeks planning and then got up and running with remote learning. They had made sure every family had a computer and internet access and worked out a schedule so that different grades met with teachers at different times to allow for the fact that not all families had more than one device. They were working on developing videos and lessons and trying to make sure their students didn't miss out too much.

"The creativity, the commitment, the dedication on the part of teachers just continues to build as we become more comfortable and understanding the possibilities that can be done through remote learning," Stirling said in mid-April.

"You're literally put into a situation where what you used to know to be the normal is no longer available and you're creating the normal as you go along day by day," he said.

We Can All Get Smarter

In terms of outward appearances there is not much to connect the districts I have profiled in this book.

- Chicago, Illinois
- Steubenville, Ohio
- Lane, Oklahoma
- Cottonwood, Oklahoma
- Seaford, Delaware
- Valley Stream 30, New York

They are wildly different in terms of size, demographics, locale, available resources, and lots of other ways. But each one in some way breaks the correlation between students' background and achievement. That is to say, they all serve students of color and students from low-income backgrounds and they are all high achieving or rapidly improving.

To find them, I followed the advice of Ronald Edmonds: "First you identify schools that produce the outcomes you're interested in. Then you watch them and try to figure out what makes them different from ineffective schools."[1] He was talking about schools, and in this book I am looking at districts, but the principle is the same. The outcome I was interested in was academic achievement of students of color and students living in poverty, and the districts I profile in this book are clear outliers.

The question is, what about them makes them more effective than other similar districts?

It would be nice if we could discern one easily identifiable factor—or even two or three. Maybe it's passionate, hard-working teachers like Natalie Campana in Steubenville; a coherent reading program like Bookworms in Seaford; a particular set of assessments or student management programs; or maybe a particular grant program.

As nice as it would be to boil the success of these districts down to a couple of those things, I don't think the answer lies in that direction. After all, there are plenty of passionate, hard-working teachers in ineffective districts, and the same can be said about good reading programs, assessments, data systems, and grant programs.

What distinguishes these districts isn't anything that easy. Rather, I think it is an "ethos," to use the word Sir Michael Rutter used to describe effective schools in 1979.[2] What does that ethos consist of? It's hard to beat Ronald Edmonds's phrase: a culture in which "it is incumbent on all personnel to be instructionally effective for all pupils."[3]

Let's look at Edmonds's words a little bit closer.

- "Incumbent" is nicely deployed here, implying that all the adults have internalized the responsibility to ensure that kids get smarter, but with the additional implication that there is some unspecified accountability for doing so.
- The words "all personnel" signify that making kids smarter is not the sole responsibility of individual teachers, but rather of all the teaching staff and indeed all the adults in the building, from the cafeteria folks to the bus drivers to the librarians, counselors, principals, and superintendents. That isn't to say teachers are unimportant; rather, that teachers are part of a larger team that is responsible for results.
- "Instructionally effective" is a broad description of all that is necessary to make kids smarter—curriculum, schedules, materials, pedagogy, intervention, engagement, encouragement—but without specifying any particular approach. Other words of Edmonds's are apropos here—"Fortunately, children know how to learn in more ways than we know how to teach, thus permitting great latitude in choosing instructional strategy."

- And, finally, the words "all pupils." Edmonds bitingly wrote, "Schools teach those they think they must and when they think they needn't, they don't." His work specifically focused on children who lived in poverty and African American children, and so when he talked about *all* children he meant the children whom schools too often "think they needn't" teach—children of color, particularly African American children, and children living in poverty.

All the districts in this book—and, I should say, other effective districts and schools I have written about in the past—are filled with adults who feel it incumbent on themselves to be instructionally effective for all kids.

But what does that mean in more concrete terms?

1. Leadership

Each of the districts has school and district leaders who believe in the capacity of schools to make kids smarter and who work relentlessly to ensure that they do.

None of the leaders in this book is a fluffy, utopian idealist. All are hard-headed career educators who have seen the power schools have to change lives. As Melinda Young, superintendent of Steubenville City Schools, said, "The truth is you can really see it, and it's exciting when you see the breakthroughs." They all know, as she said, that they can "change the path of poverty."

Not only that, but they know they are the ones who can. They aren't waiting for the cavalry to teach the kids; they are the cavalry.[4]

That doesn't mean they think it is easy to educate all children. In fact, they know it isn't. So they have had to think hard about how to lead improvement. And what they have all realized is that that process comes down to lots of people learning to make better decisions over time.

Even in small districts, adults make thousands—millions—of independent decisions every day. Decisions such as how to greet students, how to talk with parents, how to communicate within schools, how to explain a math problem, how to establish a bus route, how to serve breakfast, how to read a book aloud, which books to assign students to read, and on and on. The decisions are endless, and each one is part of creating the culture of a school and helping students get smarter. There is no way to control all those decisions, nor should leaders want to. Instead, the school and district leaders in this book see their job as helping "all personnel" to make better decisions over time. And that means that they provide a clear vision and then work on ensuring that all the adults get the information they need to make better decisions in service of that vision. Decisions flow from culture, not control.

Teri Brecheen's vision was simple: no student will leave Cottonwood without knowing how to read. Teachers were initially wary of such a vision; accustomed to many students failing to learn how to read, they couldn't see how that could change, especially given the difficult circumstances many of their students live in. But Brecheen shared with teachers the research on how children learn to read; she brought in a better reading program; she demonstrated how students could be successful. And over time Cottonwood's teachers became such expert reading teachers that they were able to help the teachers of Lane become expert reading teachers.

The initial animating vision that began Steubenville's improvement process was similar to Cottonwood's: no fourth-grade student should fail the state reading test and have to repeat fourth grade. They brought in a program that addressed every aspect of reading instruction and provided intensive help for any child who needed it. They continually studied their results and adjusted their practices in light of their results. Today, one of the poorest cities in Ohio competes with some of the wealthiest districts in the country.

The clear vision Dave Perrington brought to Seaford was "equity." That, is, the idea that *all* students would be able to meet state standards, not just some of the middle-class white kids. After putting in place a clear reading curriculum that addressed all aspects of reading instruction and also supplying assessments, and then providing principals and teachers with the opportunities to continually study the results and adjust instructional practices in light of those results, today one of the poorest districts in Delaware is the fastest improving and is on track to becoming one of the top performing. It is notable that all groups of students, including white kids, are improving, but the groups that were furthest behind—African American students, English language learners, and students with disabilities—are improving fastest.

The leaders I write about in these districts don't expect principals, teachers, and staff members to know everything necessary to make kids smarter; they do expect them to be curious and willing to learn, improve, and lead efforts to find solutions to problems. Perrington looked for people who say, "I want to get better and I can get better at what it is that I'm doing." And when teachers or other staff members didn't show they were interested in getting better—that is, if they did not feel it incumbent upon themselves to be instructionally effective, he brought a sense of urgency to the question. "Your role is so important here that we can't afford to have someone who's not doing what they need to be doing for our students."

But note what this approach doesn't do. It doesn't blame principals and teachers for student failure. It requires that, when students fail, something needs to change. But this doesn't entail blaming adults for that failure. Blame falls only on adults who refuse responsibility for thinking about what else they can learn and what else they can try.

It is notable that all the districts included in this book, except Chicago, have had a continuity of district leadership for some time, which is relatively unusual among high-poverty districts. Remember, for example, that when Roland Smith arrived in low performing Lane, he was the fourth superintendent *that year.* That instability beats even Chicago, which had seven CEOs from 2009 to 2018. In many ways Chicago's improvement has been in spite of district leadership rather than because of it. Chicago's explicit commitment to decentralized leadership may have buffered the schools from harmful CEO turnover. But underneath the many turnstile superintendents has been a steady development of school and district-office leadership supported by a citywide infrastructure that has helped teachers, principals, and local school council members to make better decisions through the years. Chicago still has a very long way to go, but with Janice Jackson in the CEO seat, Chicago may have the superintendent who can lead the district to higher heights in the next few years—if the coronavirus and the attendant economic recession do not undermine its progress. (Fingers crossed.)

2. Scientific Method

In order to help adults make better decisions, the leaders in these districts all use some version of the scientific method. As Seaford superintendent Dave Perrington said, "In the other disciplines, it works—and it can work for us."

It is simple enough: Identify a problem based on evidence; propose a solution based on local data and existing research; implement it; gather data; analyze and see if the problem is solved; if so, identify the reasons and extend and expand the solution; if not, identify reasons and either adjust or start over.

"When you do that week after week, month after month, year after year, you start seeing success," as former superintendent Roland Smith of Lane, Oklahoma, said. This is not easy work. Among other things it requires educators to develop a thick skin and professional distance. Education is an intensely personal profession, and educators do things because they think they are doing the right thing. It takes real intellectual toughness to be able to say, "Hmm—I thought I was teaching x, but my students didn't learn x, so I guess I need to rethink." It is much easier to place blame for failure on students and their families' circumstances than to turn the attention back to what happens within the classroom, school, and district.

This way of working by its very nature builds leadership capacity throughout schools and districts, because ideas and solutions come from everywhere. A paraeducator's insight into why a student may be having trouble with a particular concept or skill is just as valuable as those of a teacher, principal, or superintendent. A bus driver or school secretary may have information about a student that no other professional in the building knows. A brand-new teacher might have better training in reading or math instruction than a veteran one. This is one of the reasons "Leave your egos at the door" became the mantra at Lane.

In the case of Chicago, the district's high schools galvanized around the problem of dropouts as a problem of professional practice, not as a problem residing primarily in students or their families. The UChicago Consortium provided detailed analyses and research about what contributed to students dropping out, and educators came together to posit possible solutions. And then they kept at it, looking at whether the solution worked for them in their school. If so, they continued. If not, they tried something else. They shared their successes and failures across schools and across the district. And, as president of the Chicago Teachers Union Jesse Sharkey said, "You do that over a number of years, and it takes a while to see it, but it has had an effect."

This is where the power of variation comes in. Different teachers or teams of teachers, different schools or clusters of schools will develop different hypotheses and try different solutions. And, with common metrics of success, all the adults in the district are able to see who was more successful. In this way they expose expertise and can ask what I consider to be the most powerful question in education: "Your kids are doing better than mine. What are you doing?" That is the question that launched Lane onto its improvement trajectory after the superintendent studied the state assessment data for Oklahoma and found Cottonwood. It is the question that Seaford's teachers are encouraged to ask of each other every time they meet in professional learning communities. It is the question that drives improvement.[5]

One benefit of this continual examination of data is that it allows teachers and principals to be creative and try new things, because they know there will be a backstop. If whatever they try doesn't work, it will be caught in this cycle of examination and changed before much damage can be done. But if it does work, others can learn from the expertise that has been developed and try for themselves.

I should say that most educators are good at the first part of the scientific method cycle—they are used to identifying problems, proposing, and implementing solutions. They do it all the time. The hard part—the tedious part—the part that is too rarely done—is monitoring and analyzing the data to see if the solution worked, learning, and changing in light of the evidence.

I am reminded of a time when I was speaking to a group of administrators in northern California. I asked if anyone had high rates of student mobility, and when a principal raised his hand I asked what his school did to incorporate new students into the school. He said that the school assigned student ambassadors to help orient new students to the school and make them feel more comfortable. I asked him, "Does it work?" In other words, do the new students feel oriented and comfortable? Are they able to find friend groups and places to sit at lunch? He shrugged and said that this was what they did—he didn't really know if it worked. That lack of curiosity is what keeps schools doing ineffective things year after year. The solution made sense to him, so he never bothered to follow up to see if it was successful. But human beings don't always act and react the way you think they will, even when you do something that seems perfectly sensible. It's necessary to find out what effects our actions have.

For example, I am sure there will be district leaders who read about Steubenville and Seaford and think, "We just need to adopt Success for All or Bookworms and they will solve our reading problem." And I am the first to say that districts could do a lot worse than using one of those programs, which both incorporate a lot of the existing research about how children learn to read. But programs don't solve problems. Good, well-researched programs can be useful tools for helping people solve problems, but people solve problems. And this is why folks in Steubenville and Seaford are continually evaluating whether they are getting the results they want to see. If a student isn't achieving, they aren't satisfied with saying, "Well, that's our program." They adjust what they are doing.

So, for example, Carol Leveillee, principal of Frederick Douglass Elementary School in Seaford, saw that a few of her students weren't proficient in phonics despite multiple sessions with the Bookworms program's materials. She and her teachers are trying another program, designed for students with reading disabilities, with those students. And if that doesn't work they'll think about trying something else. They aren't responsible to a program; they are responsible to children.

And this gets to the real point. The educators in these districts hold student success as the constant and vary what they do to achieve it. The reason they are willing to continually examine what they do is because they see all children as capable of success and they see themselves as responsible for making sure they succeed.

3. Systems of Support

It's all very well to say that educators should collaboratively use the scientific method. It is another thing to provide the systems that enable it.

Paul Zavitkovsky, a leadership coach at the University of Illinois at Chicago, put it this way: "The key to a high performing school is that it becomes a community where adult learning is as important as kid learning is. And because of the infrastructure of American schools . . . you're fighting an uphill battle to create the time and the space to do systematic adult learning where adults can really learn their way through chronic problems together."

Fighting that uphill battle is a key role for school and district leaders, and the districts in this book do so in a number of different ways:

a. Managing time

Teachers and principals need time when they are not responsible for children to sit together with assessment data, behavioral data, attendance data, student work—whatever information they think can help them answer the question of how to help their students get smarter. Too many people seem to think that the only time that teachers are working is the time teachers are in front of children. But in order to work effectively they need time together with the other adults in the building to think deeply about the effects of what they are doing, what they should do more of and what they should do less of.

They also need time when they can provide students with whatever extra help students need. So, for example, Lane has "Eagle Time" when small groups of students meet with an adult to work on a specific weakness they have, whether it is vowel digraphs or morphology. Similarly, Valley Stream 30 sets aside two periods in their eight-period day for intervention and enrichment so that every student gets whatever extra help they might need and also has an opportunity to do something extra, whether it is building something or writing a play, that enriches their classroom experience.

b. Managing data

In the case of assessment data, teachers need to be looking at how students did on the same assessment given at roughly the same time. Sometimes this is state assessment data but more often it is classroom formative assessment data, which requires that teachers have to have agreed on what students should be learning and when. It doesn't mean, by the way, that they have to agree on *how* to teach. By trying out different methods, teachers, teams of teachers, and whole schools can develop the variations that are so valuable in moving the profession forward.

But without common data there is no real way to expose and learn from expertise. Test score data isn't the only important data—suspensions and expulsions, attendance, grades, graduation rates, college-going rates, college remediation rates, parent and student perceptions of the school experience—all provide important information that exposes expertise that school, district, and state leaders can learn from. But it is important to focus on the data that is core to the problems schools and districts are trying to solve and not drown in all the data it is possible to assemble.

c. Building a culture of trust

As I've said, teachers, principals, and superintendents have to be able to say: "Your kids are doing better than mine—what are you doing?" That question jumpstarts improvement. But simply to ask that question betrays vulnerability. In order to reveal their weakness, educators need to work within a culture of trust where professionals acknowledge that they don't know everything and need help. It is long past time to acknowledge that it is impossible for individual educators to know all there is to know about making kids smarter—there is simply too much to know. It is only by pooling their knowledge and learning from expertise that educators can possibly expect to help all kids. And that means they need to trust that their vulnerabilities will not be used against them but, rather, demonstrate what more they need to learn. "The best thing you can do is say, 'I don't know, but I'm willing to learn and I'm willing to find it out,'" is the way Lane's current superintendent, Pam Matthews, puts it. "There's nothing wrong with not knowing. What's wrong is if you don't find out and learn."

d. Understanding what research has established about how children learn

I said in the introduction that an awful lot of education research consists of big correlational studies and studies of individual programs and practices. But there is another body of research that should be informing educators but too often doesn't, and it has to do with how people learn. The research I referred to most in this book along these lines is the research on how children learn how to read, but there are other bodies of research about how children learn math and how they learn at all. Much of this research has been done in fields other than in education—they have been in neuroscience, cognitive science, and psychology.[6] For the most part educators in the districts I have profiled in this book have discovered many of the principles of how children learn by trial and error and through the research on reading rather than by any formal study of cognitive science principles. In that way they are demonstrating the power of holding to high expectations and doggedly working their way through the scientific method, though I can't help but think the process would be more efficient if their education programs had equipped them with some of the basic principles about how people learn.

e. **Understanding that the work is never done**

Once a district has fully incorporated the scientific method, it becomes clear that this work is never done. There is always another problem to solve, more opportunities to provide children, better ways of doing things, higher standards to reach. Steubenville isn't resting on its laurels because it graduates just about all its students; it has set a goal of having half its graduates earn some college credits before leaving high school. If it reaches that goal, it will set another one.

So, to sum up, the common elements of these districts are *leadership* that defines a vision of high expectations for all students and builds a culture where all adults in the system feel it incumbent to make kids smarter; a *process* to guide the adults in the district to making better decisions while growing their ability to do so using the scientific method; and *systems* to undergird that improvement process.

I've used some general terms where some of them were more specific, and specific ones where they were more general, but none of what I just said stands in opposition to what Rutter, Edmonds, Leithwood, the UChicago Consortium, and others have found.[7]

To boil it down further, district success does not consist of lots of random acts of education but, rather, organizing individual efforts to work together to make kids smarter.

WHY ISN'T SUCCESS MORE WIDESPREAD?

So, if what I have found isn't new and revolutionary but rooted in research that has been around at least since the 1970s, why isn't the kind of success I have documented more widespread? Honestly, this is a puzzle that I don't know that anyone can fully explain.

But a few things go part of the way to an explanation.

It's Hard to Translate Research into Practice

It is one thing to say that school and district organization, not individual effort, drives improvement. It's another thing to organize schools and districts in ways that help them improve. Decades after we got rid of most one-room schoolhouses we still organize our schools around the isolated, idiosyncratic practices of individual teachers. Changing organizational structure—and the way people work—is hard.

Here's a rather simple example from the medical field. Doctors have known since the 1840s that unless they wash their hands between patients they are likely to spread infection. And yet, study after study demonstrates that it is very hard to get doctors to wash their hands. One reason is that hospitals weren't organized around handwashing, so—especially in older buildings—sinks, soap, and towels aren't always easily available. But even when such hospitals provide alcohol disinfectant—that is, change their structure—doctors don't always change their practice and sanitize their hands. Whether they do so seems to largely depend on whether hospital leadership has established a culture in which it is incumbent on all personnel to prevent infection.[8]

Which leads to the next issue.

Most School and District Leaders Don't Know How to Learn from Others in Order to Improve

This has two parts to it:

1) MANY EDUCATORS RESIST THE IDEA THAT OTHERS HAVE SOMETHING TO TEACH THEM There is a tradition in education that says that every classroom, every school, every district is peculiarly different from every other classroom, school, and district. Principals whose students are primarily African American often feel they can't learn from principals whose students are primarily Hispanic—and vice versa. Superintendents in suburban districts often feel they can't learn from those in cities or rural areas. I was both amused and dismayed when I heard that a principal of a rather middling-achieving school said examples of high performing high-poverty schools held no lessons for her because she had *too few* students who lived in poverty.

In this book and my previous books, I have worked to ensure representation of different locales, sizes, and demographics to reduce those kinds of objections. But to learn from them educators need to shift their understanding to allow for the idea that it is possible to generalize lessons from other schools and districts. Kids are kids; schools are schools. Success and improvement hold lessons for anyone willing to look at the data and say: "Your students are doing better than mine. What are you doing?" That doesn't mean that simply adopting some program or practice of a higher performer will automatically lead to higher performance. But success often has lessons that can be adapted to other contexts.

2) MOST SCHOOL AND DISTRICT LEADERS DON'T UNDERSTAND HOW TO LEAD IMPROVEMENT AT ALL
Because we as a nation have underestimated the knowledge, skill, and resources necessary to make all kids smarter, we have allowed our schools and districts to be led by people who, too often, don't understand how to organize schools and districts to marshal the full power of institutions.

This is a solvable problem. If we were to take seriously the complexity of the job and provided the kind of knowledge and training principals and superintendents need, we could have the school and district leaders we need.

There are different ways to approach this. The University of Illinois at Chicago trains principals who lead more improvement than the district posts as a whole. And UIC has been at the work long enough that some of its graduates—most notably Chicago's current CEO—have gone on to district-level leadership. But UIC's approach is not the only possibility; other universities are working on improving their principal preparation programs, and we should be able to see over time if their approaches are equally or more successful. The Wallace Foundation funded six large and diverse districts to develop comprehensive pipelines of principal preparation—from recruitment to training to hiring, placement, and support. Each has a slightly different approach, each has a different kind of relationship with higher education institutions. But, overall, they have demonstrated that better principal preparation and support can lead to more student success.[9] Other districts have different ways of deliberately building a leadership corps. In other words, we know of a variety of ways to prepare better principals and superintendents, and over time we should be able to learn from the variations what works best in what contexts.

But the point is that the knowledge and skill of educators who can lead effective schools and districts—like the ones documented in this book—can be developed.

I should note that the educators in the districts I have profiled, for the most part, look very similar to educators everywhere, with similar career trajectories and backgrounds. They are doing extraordinary work not because of their personal characteristics or backgrounds but because they know in their bones that kids can get smarter and they have learned, often through trial and error, how to work together to marshal the full power of schools and districts to help them do so.

If they can do this work, others can as well. We know that ordinary people can learn to do extraordinary things. It is up to the nation to muster the political will and resources necessary to ensure that all our principals and superintendents are capable of leading the work we need them to do. And that takes us to the next issue.

We as a Nation Have Not Fully Committed to Making All Kids Smarter

It is hard to muster the political will necessary to make all schools and districts effective when not everyone *wants* to make all kids smarter.

Our founding document, the Declaration of Independence, declares that all people

> are created equal, that they are endowed by their Creator with certain unalienable Rights, that among these are Life, Liberty and the pursuit of Happiness. That to secure these rights, governments are instituted among men, deriving their just powers from the consent of the governed.[10]

Most proponents of democracy agree that for the governed to provide their consent requires public schools to prepare all children to become educated citizens who can weigh in on the kind of country we will have, the institutions we build, and the issues we tackle locally and nationally.

But the United States has spent more than two hundred years deciding whether our founding ideals of equality or our founding realities of inequality would prevail.[11]

Both traditions can be found throughout the history of American schooling. Sometimes schools serve as the mechanism by which ordinary children, with no connections to wealth and power, are able to rise to positions of great public and private responsibility; other times they consign the most eager and excited learners to preordained pathways to powerlessness.[12]

The wheat-from-chaff sorting role has been profound, and its effects have been felt by many children who too often have been seen as the chaff—African American children, Native American children, Hispanic children, and children from low-income and working backgrounds. This was institutionalized for much of the twentieth century, for example, in schools that openly and unapologetically triaged students—one-third were prepared for college, one-third for business careers, one-third for vocational careers. The bottom two tracks often consisted of simply holding kids in schools until they got old enough to work.[13] "Poor student, little chance" was written on the permanent record of Richard Ranallo's father, meaning that as the son of an Italian millworker, he was not seen as a student worthy of effort. His was far from a unique experience.

In the 1980s, many high schools ended formal tracks and their vocational programs, but never figured out how to adjust to the new expectation that they would actually educate all kids. In fact, some educators steeped in this school of thought deeply resent the idea that they are expected to make all kids smarter. They might or might not know how to help the top third of kids get into college, but that seems like a reasonable mission to them. They throw their hands up at the thought of educating all kids.

But the educating-for-democracy tradition has also had a long legacy in American public schools, and I would argue that the educators I have written about in this and previous books are part of it. Many educators throughout the country are fully committed to the notion that their job is to educate all their students and work hard to make that a reality. They have kept alive the ideal of equality for all and have inspired many a panegyric by former students about how profoundly their lives were changed by their teachers.

The two visions for schools are in continual tension.

But here's the real rub.

Not Everyone Agrees That All Kids Can Get Smarter

Ronald Edmonds had a lot to say about this topic:

> A very great proportion of the American people believe that family background and home environment are principal causes of the quality of pupil performance. In fact, no notion about schooling is more widely held than the belief that the family is somehow the principal determinant of whether or not a child will do well in school. The popularity of that belief continues partly because many social scientists and opinion makers continue to espouse the belief that family background is chief cause of the quality of pupil performance.

He finished up that paragraph with a killer sentence:

> Such a belief has the effect of absolving educators of their professional responsibility to be instructionally effective.

Because most schools haven't really been organized to make the individual efforts of teachers successful, even educators who began their careers believing they could make their students smarter sometimes become discouraged as their efforts dissipate. They work hard and do what is expected of them, and yet their students don't achieve.

Unaware of the power they could be wielding if schools were organized differently, educators too often have turned to what the Coleman report and its descendants seem to say: that there is something wrong with the kids. As longtime Seaford teacher Tammy Steele said of Seaford before Dave Perrington arrived as superintendent, "There was a lot of blaming." This plays out in painful detail in schools and districts where educators do not understand how to teach children to read.

Teaching all children to read, as I talk about throughout the book, requires a lot of knowledge and skill on the part of teachers. It can be done, but if teachers don't understand the complexity they can easily fall into the trap of thinking that some children are simply incapable of learning to read.[14] And the older kids get without learning to read, the more obdurate, unmotivated, and disengaged they become, giving rise to the idea that they don't want to learn. School power dynamics being what they are, worried white parents are more likely to have their demands for help answered; wealthier, educated parents are more likely get their children outside help. Those realities mean that students of color and students from low-income families, who are more reliant on schools, have higher rates of reading failure.

Any beginning student of statistics can say that correlation is not causation, but seeing endless demonstrations of the correlation between socioeconomic status and academic achievement has pushed many people into believing that there is a causal relationship between them. Some who cite the correlational studies deny vehemently that they themselves are prejudiced against children from low-income backgrounds and children of color; rather, they consider that they are expressing sympathy with children who are facing obstacles that are unconscionable in the richest nation on earth. The effect of their words, however, is to join forces with open racists who question whether children of color and children who live in poverty are capable of getting smarter.

This is where examples of outliers should be valuable; they demonstrate that it is possible for schools to break the correlation between socioeconomic status and achievement. Here again is Edmonds:

> How many effective schools would you have to see to be persuaded
> of the educability of poor children? If the answer is more than one, I
> submit that you have reasons of your own to believe that basic pupil
> performance derives from family background rather than school re-
> sponse to family background.[15]

Edmonds was, of course, referring to the deep race and class prejudice that permeates the United States. Such prejudice conflicts with the story the nation likes to tell itself that ours is a nation that doesn't see race and class but allows talent, wherever it exists, to rise equally. Edmonds, an African American educator from Ypsilanti, Michigan, understood that schools were as much enforcers of prejudice as breakers of it, and he provided a way for the education world to learn from outliers that would confront those prejudices.

But for outliers to provide that existence proof, they have to be known to exist.

Most of the examples in this book are small districts and, you could argue, somewhat obscure. I thought Steubenville might have caught the interest of Ohio education professors, but when I called a bunch of them, they were politely baffled that I would think to ask them if they or their colleagues had spent any time trying to figure out why one of the highest poverty districts in their state was also one of the highest achieving.

But Chicago is neither small nor obscure. Its improvement has been thoroughly documented by some of the most respected education researchers in the country and validated by multiple sources of data. And yet its improvement still comes as news to people who would normally be expected to pay attention to such matters. And this is where I think it is important to think about how people get their information about schools and the state of journalism today.

We Can't Learn from What We Don't Know About

In 2015, in an op-ed published in the *Chicago Tribune*, Robin Steans of the nonprofit education advocacy organization Advance Illinois and Stephanie Banchero, a former education reporter for the *Chicago Tribune* and *Wall Street Journal* who's now a program officer at the Joyce Foundation, pled with reporters to cover Chicago's improvement:

> Amid the frequently facile national caricature of Chicago as homicide central, political corruption run amok and terrible schools, there is a nuanced tale of educational momentum. The fact that this storyline gets drowned out by the intense fascination with failure does a disservice to students, teachers and the national conversation about school improvement.[16]

Their plea went largely unanswered.

The question is why?

After all, a huge, politically dysfunctional district, despite being perennially starved of resources, has slowly, steadily made improvements that helped more kids learn and find their way through high school and into college at rates that are very comparable to the rest of the country. How is that not a major story?

Much of the country has been denuded of local journalism, which is a separate tragedy that deserves its own conversation. But Chicago still has a robust local press that the national press pays attention to. So why has it not addressed the improvement of Chicago's schools in a concerted way that would attract national attention?

Part of the answer lies in the fact that reporters are by their nature skeptical. When Sean Reardon presented his findings at a conference of education writers, one of the Chicago reporters in the room said quite simply, "We don't believe it." She was thinking, she told me later, about all the many stresses the school system had been under in the years Reardon was analyzing—years with a major teacher strike, superintendent malfeasance, and fights with the state over continued underfunding. How could students have moved forward in those years? It didn't make sense to her.

And there is no question that CPS still has enormous problems. The fourth-largest district in the country has plenty of failure and dysfunction that needs to be talked about and fixed. That fact means that she and other reporters also reflexively react against the kind of boosterism typical of mayors and superintendents. Former Mayor Rahm Emanuel, for example, claimed that by closing forty-nine neighborhood schools that mostly served African American students he had helped strengthen the overall system. Knowing how much disruption, anger, and unhappiness the school closures had caused, Emanuel's boasts just got reporters' backs up and they barely listened to subsequent information from the mayor and CEO. When Janice Jackson arrived at the district office she was surprised by the level of distrust with which she was greeted. "It was a bit shocking to be in this position where people don't necessarily believe what you're saying—because as a principal you just enjoy a great degree of trust with the community," she said. For this reason, Jackson pushed for the word "integrity" to be incorporated into the district's vision. "Until we have established more public trust, I don't know if people are going to embrace it the way that we want them to. But that doesn't mean we're going to stop telling the story, spreading the good news."

Another piece of why more journalists have not dug into Chicago's improvement is that it is difficult to capture. I should say that there's plenty about Chicago that I have not talked about—it's a big, complex system, and no book chapter could possibly include everything important. What that means is that there's nothing that journalists would call sexy about Chicago's improvement—no easily identifiable program or charismatic superintendent who fixed things. In fact, the improvement is largely in spite of the turnstile superintendents, rather than because of them. The complexity of the story means that, as one of Chicago's best education reporters told me, if she went to her editor to say she was going to do a story on why CPS has improved, "She'd say, 'Good luck with that.'"

Those reasons partly explain why Chicago's improvement hasn't made its way into the national consciousness, though there have been sporadic attempts to at least mention them.[17]

But I think there is something deeper at work. Many journalists—myself included—have been trained to think of themselves as being part of a system of holding institutions accountable but who should not have any political allegiances.[18] The idea is that any kind of political adherence would somehow taint reporters' ability to report fairly and objectively.[19] In its extreme form this means filtering out even a loyalty to democracy itself.[20] This has created a journalistic corps that, while it exposes failures in public institutions, otherwise recounts events in a neutral way. Conservatives have used those failures as a battering ram against the very idea of public institutions. Ronald Reagan's secretary of education William Bennett, after all, had no real ideas for improving Chicago's public schools when he excoriated them. He instead proposed undoing them altogether by instituting a citywide tuition voucher program. President Donald Trump's secretary of education's proposals for the nation's schools amounted to the same thing, referring to public schools with the contemptuous phrase she helped make popular, "government schools."

This raises the question of why conservatives are hostile to public institutions and the taxes that fund them. Not all conservatives have traditionally had contempt for public institutions, of course. But the conservative movement as it exists in 2020 has made it clear that its primary goal is to cut taxes and gut all government services except the military and law enforcement.

This is where I think it important to remember what happened after Reconstruction in the South. In addition to establishing the Ku Klux Klan and other paramilitary groups, antidemocratic counterrevolutionaries declared the schools that the freedmen had established during Reconstruction were unnecessary and, furthermore, that the taxes imposed to fund schools were confiscatory and oppressive. They burned schools, murdered educators, and ended school taxes, ensuring that the South would remain a more or less feudal oligarchy with an uneducated and terrorized population incapable of mounting a sustained political challenge for many decades.[21]

It is easy to see this as white supremacy and entrenchment of institutional racism. But if anything can be a deeper force than racism, it might be the animus against democracy, an animus that uses racism as a way to divide natural allies. Schools established by the African American politicians who briefly held elected office after the Civil War were for all children—white, Black, and Native. White Southern oligarchs, who privately educated their own children, both inflamed and exploited the racism of poor white people in order to divide them from people with whom they had a common interest.

Democratically controlled public institutions, with all their balkiness and faults, exist to serve all. But the current conservative movement, with its endemic hostility to taxes and public education, paints public institutions as parasites. If this were any other country, we would know to call this brand of conservatism antidemocratic. However, reporters who have been enculturated into traditions of political objectivity report on conservatives' actions and rhetoric in a neutral fashion while continuing to focus on institutional failure.

Mainstream reporters who do not publicly and openly acknowledge their role as cocreators of democracy allow journalism to be used as a weapon in the dismantling of democracy. This means reporters are complicit in creating political conditions that undermine journalism. After all, agents of healthy democracies do not call reporters "enemies of the state," nor do they murder them.

Chicago's story thus poses a challenge to American journalism. Chicago is a clear example of a piece-by-piece rebuilding of a massive public institution, with more improvement than any other large school district. In many ways it represents a triumph of democracy that can give heart to all those who fear that America can no longer solve problems and aspire to big things.

But its story has largely gone untold. And I suspect that because Chicago's school system is so connected in the public mind with African American children as well as African American teachers and principals, the public will continue to be suspicious of any news of improvement. Even Americans who don't consider themselves to be racist openly doubt that a system serving primarily children of color from low-income backgrounds and taught and led by educators of color can improve in any substantial way. That the largest student enrollment group in Chicago is now Hispanic will not be likely to change minds about a district that is more than 80 percent Black and brown.

And this means that the nation is allowing racism to blind it to pathways forward in improving schools.

We as a nation pay a heavy price for the racist structures and ways of thinking that were built into our foundations and continue today; our inability to learn from Chicago is just one example. We may tell ourselves that we have a commitment to the idea that ordinary people are the best repository of political wisdom, and that all our fates are intertwined. But that means we need to be open to the lessons our fellow citizens have to teach us. To learn them, we will have to consciously confront the ways that racism and antidemocratic forces have undermined our willingness to do so.

The Intertwined Struggle for Democracy and Public Education

I began this book saying that we have schools to make kids smarter and that smarter kids—kids who understand science, know history, and have pondered the nature of existence by being exposed to great literature, art, and philosophy—grow up to be citizens who extend, sustain, and expand democracy.

As I write this, at the end of 2020, pro-democracy and antidemocracy forces are battling to see who will prevail in the United States. Even as antidemocratic forces attempt to limit the number of people who can vote, they seek to weaken and dismantle public schools—as they have in the past.

This time, however, antidemocracy forces can count on a certain kind of pessimism about public schools. That is, even some who are staunchly pro-democracy have become discouraged about whether public schools *can* do much to help kids become smart. Others have become convinced that schools *can* but *won't*.

These twin pessimisms may strike such a heavy blow that even if we as a nation preserve the ability of ordinary people to have a say in how we are governed, public education may be severely weakened. And that will further attenuate our ability to secure self-rule.

I wrote this book hoping to counter such pessimism. The districts I have profiled in this book provide clear arguments against the idea that public schools are incapable of improvement and excellence. They demonstrate that our future fellow citizens—children from all backgrounds—are capable of getting smarter and that the efforts of ordinary educators, when marshaled together, can help them do so.

Kids can get smarter.

We can all get smarter.

We just have to muster the will to do so.

Notes

INTRODUCTION

1. Karin Chenoweth, *It's Being Done: Academic Success in Unexpected Schools* (Cambridge, MA: Harvard Education Press, 2007).
2. Karin Chenoweth, *Schools That Succeed: How Educators Marshal the Power of Systems for Improvement* (Cambridge, MA: Harvard Education Press, 2017).
3. Mel Ainscow, *Towards Self-Improving School Systems: Lessons from a City Challenge* (New York: Routledge, 2015).
4. James Coleman et al., *Equality of Educational Opportunity* (Washington, DC: National Center for Educational Statistics, 1966), https://files.eric.ed.gov /fulltext/ED012275.pdf. By *achievement,* Coleman basically meant the ability to pass tests that measured mathematical reasoning, vocabulary, reading comprehension, and general knowledge that included the practical arts, both "male" and "female." That is to say, the tests he used to judge achievement were probably worth critiquing.
5. Richard Herrnstein and Charles Murray, *The Bell Curve: Intelligence and Class Structure in American Life* (New York: Free Press, 1994).
6. My previous books have documented such examples, but there are many more.
7. This information is from the long-term NAEP, https://nces.ed.gov/nations reportcard/pubs/main2012/2013456.aspx#section1 (accessed 9.21.19).
8. Whenever I think about this I think of the 1967 movie *To Sir, with Love* with Sidney Poitier. I don't really know if it represents a realistic picture of the London high schools involved, but it does give me a visual image. If you haven't seen the movie, it's a classic of the teacher-as-hero genre.
9. Michael Rutter, *Fifteen Thousand Hours* (Cambridge, MA: Harvard University Press, 1982).
10. Michael Rutter and Barbara Vaughan, "School Effectiveness Findings, 1979–2002," *Journal of School Psychology*, 40, no. 6 (November–December 2002): 451–475, doi: 10.1016/S0022-4405(02)00124-3.

11. Ronald R. Edmonds, "Effective Schools for the Urban Poor," *Educational Leadership* 37, no. 1 (October 1979): 15–24, https://pdfs.semanticscholar.org/55ob/74oeb13c411d36d38f498293472cf64fdcef.pdf.

12. Ron Brandt, "On School Improvement: A Conversation with Ronald Edmonds," *Educational Leadership* 40, no. 3 (December 1982), http://www.ascd.org/ASCD/pdf/journals/ed_lead/el_198212_brandt2.pdf.

13. One of the most frustrating parts of research on individual programs and practices is that even when the research points to something really effective, that research is often ignored. The prime example of this is Project Follow Through, which was a nine-year federal government study beginning in 1968 that compared 22 models of instruction in schools serving 200,000 students. It was a huge study that found that only one model raised academic achievement, and the affected students had more confidence and self-esteem. That model was Direct Instruction, which is a highly scripted program where teachers directly and explicitly teach children a careful sequence of knowledge and skills. The results of Project Follow Through were buried, and few people have even heard of it.

14. Anthony S. Bryk et al., *Organizing Schools for Improvement: Lessons from Chicago* (Chicago: University of Chicago Press, 2010).

15. William Bennett, "The Future of Education in America," (talk at the Cato Institute, Washington, DC, August 30, 1988), https://www.c-span.org/video/?4422-1/future-education-america.

16. Kenneth Leithwood et al., *How Leadership Influences Student Learning* (New York: Wallace Foundation, 2004), https://www.wallacefoundation.org/knowledge-center/Documents/How-Leadership-Influences-Student-Learning.pdf.

17. Brandt, "On School Improvement."

CHAPTER 1

1. In 2016 Maryland's governor Larry Hogan, for example, issued an executive order that Maryland schools had to wait until after Labor Day to start the fall semester. This allowed the state's tourism industry to count on more families spending Labor Day weekend at the beach.

2. I am borrowing the idea of exposing and learning from expertise from Mel Ainscow of the University of Manchester.

3. Karin Chenoweth, *Schools That Succeed: How Educators Marshal the Power of Systems for Improvement* (Cambridge, MA: Harvard Education Press, 2017).

4. Karin Chenoweth, *It's Being Done: Academic Success in Unexpected Schools* (Cambridge, MA: Harvard Education Press, 2007).

5. Karin Chenoweth, *HOW It's Being Done: Urgent Lessons from Unexpected Schools* (Cambridge, MA: Harvard Education Press, 2009).

6. Ron Brandt, "On School Improvement: A Conversation with Ronald Edmonds," *Educational Leadership* 40, no. 3 (December 1982), http://www.ascd .org/ASCD/pdf/journals/ed_lead/el_198212_brandt2.pdf.

7. Motoko Rich, Amanda Cox, and Matthew Bloch, "Money, Race, and Success: How Your District Compares," *Upshot* (blog), *New York Times*, April 29, 2016, https://www.nytimes.com/interactive/2016/04/29/upshot/money -race-and-success-how-your-school-district-compares.html.

8. Many low-income communities now offer free lunch to all their students as part of the community eligibility program. While this is absolutely the best thing for kids, it makes it more difficult for researchers to understand what percentage of children come from low-income backgrounds. The fact that Reardon is using the US Census Community Survey moves us away from a problematic source of data to a more reliable one.

9. This is not the most extreme example I could have used.

10. The first iteration of my look at districts was a podcast, *ExtraOrdinary Districts*. To hear voices of some of the people featured in this book, go to www.edtrust.org/extraordinary-districts/.

CHAPTER 2

1. Emily Badger and Kevin Quealy, "How Effective Is Your School District? A New Measure Shows Where Students Learn the Most," *New York Times*, December 5, 2017, https://www.nytimes.com/interactive/2017/12/05 /upshot/a-better-way-to-compare-public-schools.html.

2. Main NAEP has other assessments that are less frequent, but I'm just talking about the reading and math here.

3. That's one percentage point ahead of the nation; 66 percent of US eighth graders met basic reading standards in 2015. National Center for Education Statistics, "Reading Performance," *The Condition of Education 2020* (Washington, DC: Institute of Education Sciences, May 2020), https://nces.ed .gov/programs/coe/pdf/coe_cnb.pdf.

4. Jenny Nagaoka and Alex Seeskin, *The Educational Attainment of Chicago Public Schools Students: 2018* (Chicago: UChicago Consortium on School Research, November 2019), https://consortium.uchicago.edu/sites/default/files/2019-11 /CCSR%20DAI%202018%20Snapshot%20-%20FINAL_0.pdf.

5. "Illinois Report Card: 2018–2019," Illinois State Board of Education, 2019, https://www.illinoisreportcard.com/.

6. Paul Zavitkovsky and Steven Tozer, *Upstate/Downstate: Changing Patterns of Achievement, Demographics, and School Effectiveness in Illinois Public Schools under NCLB* (Chicago: Center for Urban Education Leadership, University of Illinois at Chicago, 2017), https://urbanedleadership.org/wp-content /uploads/2020/02/UPSTATE-DOWNSTATE-FINAL-w-Appendices -06.16.17.pdf.

7. I discuss this in the Conclusion.
8. Maureen Kelleher, "Chicago Schools: Worst in the Nation?" *Chicago Reporter*, November 13, 2015.
9. William Bennett, "The Future of Education in America" (talk at the Cato Institute, Washington, DC, August 30, 1988), https://www.c-span.org/video /?4422-1/future-education-america.
10. *Dropouts from the Chicago Public Schools: An Analysis of the Classes of 1982, 1983, 1984* (Chicago: Chicago Panel on Public School Finances, April 1985), https://files.eric.ed.gov/fulltext/ED258095.pdf.
11. Later a nonteacher staff member was added.
12. "History of Chicago Public Schools," *Chicago Reporter*, 2015, https://www .chicagoreporter.com/cps-history/. Another valuable resource is Elizabeth Todd-Breland, *A Political Education: Black Politics and Education Reform in Chicago Since the 1960s* (Chapel Hill: University of North Carolina Press, 2018).
13. Many states, for example, reported graduation rates as the percentage of seniors in high school who graduated. That meant they could report in the high 90 percents, because most students drop out before senior year.
14. Linda Lenz, "A Conversation with Fred Hess," *Chicago Reporter*, February 22, 2006, https://www.chicagoreporter.com/webextra-conversation-fred -hess/.
15. Interview with the author, May 2017.
16. Interview with the author, October 2016.
17. G. Alfred Hess—who was one of many who had pushed for the original reform bill—had laid some of the groundwork, along with Don Moore of Designs for Change. They knew it wasn't enough to do something that seemed like a good idea. Hess wanted to know: "Do we have evidence that kids are learning more, and can we connect that evidence to specific causes in ways that are justifiable rather than ideological?"
    Then serving as executive director of the Chicago Panel on Public School Policy and Finance, Hess studied the effects of the first few years of school reform. The first years were disappointing. On average, student achievement dropped as measured by a standardized test that Chicago administered to students, the Iowa Test of Basic Skills. The results had enough ambiguity—for example, there were different versions of the test—that it was hard to know exactly what the story was, but it was clear the LSCs hadn't immediately ushered in a golden age of improved student achievement. Hess did brief case studies of fourteen schools that showed that some schools dropped, some improved, and some stayed the same. He observed that the difference seemed to have less to do with the local school councils than with the principals. This was kind of intriguing, because until then few scholars—other than Ronald Edmonds and Michael Rutter in the 1970s— had focused on principals as a factor in school improvement.

Hess became one of a large number of community representatives who helped shape the Consortium's research agenda.

18. It also received funding from the Spencer Foundation, which supports a lot of education research—including the work of Sean Reardon.

19. "The Annenberg Challenge," Annenberg Foundation, https://annenberg.org/initiatives/education/annenberg-challenge/.

20. Mark A. Smylie and Stacy A. Wenzel, *The Chicago Annenberg Challenge: Successes, Failures, and Lessons for the Future* (Chicago: UChicago Consortium on Chicago School Research, 2003), https://consortium.uchicago.edu/sites/default/files/2018-10/p62.pdf.

21. Interview with the author.

22. I once had a discussion with a frustrated education researcher who told me that if someone said they were doing research on washing machines, it would be clear that they were researching ways to improve washing machines. But education researchers, he said, do the equivalent of explaining the failure of washing machines rather than figuring out how to make them better.

23. William A. Sampson, *Chicago Charter Schools: The Hype and the Reality* (Charlotte, NC: Information Age Publishing, 2016). For this reason, I have thought of the campaign to create new schools as something of a distraction from the main story line. I should add that the Consortium's study of Chicago's charter schools found that on average they somewhat outperformed the district schools, but the study also found so much variation that it concluded that "school type does not determine school quality." Julia A. Gwynne and Paul T. Moore, *Chicago's Charter High Schools: Organizational Features, Enrollment, School Transfers, and Student Performance* (Chicago: UChicago Consortium on School Research, 2017), https://consortium.uchicago.edu/sites/default/files/2018-10/Chicagos%20Charter%20High%20Schools-Nov2017-Consortium.pdf.

24. Chicago rather annoyingly has two top officials with the title CEO—Chief Executive Officer and Chief Education Officer.

25. Interview with the author, June 2017.

26. Anthony Bryk et al., *Charting School Reform: Democratic Localism as a Lever for Change* (Boulder, CO: Westview Press, 1998).

27. Interview with the author, June 2017.

28. Interview with the author, October 2016.

29. Elaine Allensworth and John Q. Easton, *The On-Track Indicator as a Predictor of High School Graduation* (Chicago: UChicago Consortium on School Research, 2005), https://consortium.uchicago.edu/sites/default/files/2018-10/p78.pdf.

30. This language very closely resembled the language used by Michael Rutter in his study from 1970 discussed in the Introduction.

31. Interview with the author, June 2017.

32. Elaine Allensworth, "Dropout Prevention: A Previously Intractable Problem Addressed Through Systems for Monitoring and Supporting Students," in *Prevention Science in School Settings: Complex Relationships and Processes*, ed. Kris Bosworth (New York: Springer, 2015), 353–70.

33. Interview with the author, May 2017.

34. Interview with the author, June 2017.

35. Anthony Bryk et al., *Organizing Schools for Improvement: Lessons from Chicago* (Chicago: University of Chicago Press, 2010).

36. William L. Sanders and Sandra P. Horn, "Research Findings from the Tennessee Value-Added Assessment System (TVAAS) Database: Implications for Educational Evaluation and Research," *Journal of Personnel Evaluation in Education* 12, no. 3 (September 1998): 247–56, doi: 10.1023/A:1008067210518.

37. For an extended discussion of the systems that undergird teaching and learning, see Karin Chenoweth, *Schools That Succeed: How Expert Educators Marshal the Power of Systems for Improvement* (Cambridge, MA: Harvard Education Press, 2017).

38. Whenever I go to a highly effective school I talk with teachers who say something like, "I wasn't a good teacher until I came here."

39. See, for example, Julie A. Marsh et al., *A Big Apple for Educators: New York City's Experiment with Schoolwide Performance Bonuses: Final Evaluation Report* (Santa Monica, CA: RAND Corporation, 2011), https://www.rand.org/pubs/monographs/MG1114.html.

40. This article from *NEA Today* lays out some of the issues: "NEA Survey: Nearly Half Of Teachers Consider Leaving Profession Due to Standardized Testing," *NEA Today* (November 2, 2014).

41. This language reflects some later refinements.

42. Interview with the author, June 2017.

43. Right around the time they starting working on answering this question, Arthur Levine, president of Teachers College at Columbia University, published a report that was scathingly critical of principal preparation programs, saying that the majority of the programs that prepare school leaders range in quality "from inadequate to poor." Arthur Levine, *Educating School Leaders* (Princeton, NJ: Education Schools Project, 2005), http://edschools.org/pdf/Final313.pdf. It is hard not to draw a direct line from that report to the fact that nationally, large percentages of sitting principals report feeling unprepared for the job. In particular they feel unprepared to lead academic improvement for students from low-income backgrounds and students of color. William R. Johnston and Christopher J. Young, *Principal and Teacher Preparation to Support the Needs of Diverse Students: National Findings from the American Educator Panels* (Santa Monica, CA: RAND Corporation, 2019), https://www.rand.org/pubs/research_reports/RR2990.html.

This may help explain the fact that Title I schools—which are by definition schools with children from low-income backgrounds and students of color—have enormous churn among principals. They often last less than three years, which is the minimum amount of time even expert principals need to register real improvement.

44. Interview with the author, June 2017.
45. For more on the components of a high-quality principal preparation program, see Linda Darling-Hammond et al., *Preparing School Leaders for a Changing World: Lessons from Exemplary Leadership Development Programs* (Stanford, CA: Stanford University, Stanford Educational Leadership Institute, 2007), https://www.wallacefoundation.org/knowledge-center/Documents/Preparing-School-Leaders-Executive-Summary.pdf; and Shelby Cosner et al., "Cultivating Exemplary School Leadership Preparation at a Research Intensive University," *Journal of Research on Leadership Education* 10, no. 1 (April 2015): 11–38, doi: 10.1177/1942775115569575.
46. Interview with the author, May 2017.
47. In 2016, The Wallace Foundation produced a series of videos to explain the changes in state policy that were made. *A Bold Move to Better Prepare Principals: The Illinois Story*, October 18, 2016, produced by Tod Lending, https://www.wallacefoundation.org/knowledge-center/pages/series -shows-how-illinois-successfully-revamped-requirements-for-principal -preparation.aspx.
48. Interview with the author.
49. Janice Jackson, "ExtraOrdinary Districts: Live!" November 18, 2019, *ExtraOrdinary Districts* podcast, https://edtrust.org/extraordinary-districts -live.
50. Robert J. Marzano, "A Guaranteed and Viable Curriculum," in *What Works in Schools* (Alexandria, VA: ASCD, 2003), http://www.ascd.org/publications /books/102271/chapters/A-Guaranteed-and-Viable-Curriculum.aspx.
51. Interview with the author, May 2017.
52. Interview with the author, May 2017.
53. To those who think the exodus of African American children from the system explains the improvement, some careful work by Reardon and Paul Zavitkovsky at UIC shows that this explanation doesn't hold water. "Progress and Promise: Chicago's Nation-Leading Educational Gains," Joyce Foundation, January 25, 2018, http://www.joycefdn.org/news/progress-and -promise-chicagos-nation-leading-educational-gains.
54. See the Conclusion for a longer discussion of this question.
55. Interview with the author, May 2017.
56. While I consider this a really good thing for Chicago's students, I continue to be amazed that somehow it falls on the school system to provide what at this point has to be considered a basic service like phone and mail service.

57. "Reward for Dirty Schools," *Chicago Sun-Times*, April 21, 2018, https:// chicago.suntimes.com/2018/4/21/18439103/reward-for-dirty-schools-259 -million-more-from-the-chicago-public-schools.
58. "Equity Talks," Discovery Education, webinar with Janice Jackson, Richard Carranza, and Susan Cordova, June 14, 2020, https://www.discovery education.com/learn/equity-talks/.
59. Janice Jackson, "May 30 Protests," *Inside CPS* (blog), June 1, 2020, https:// blog.cps.edu/2020/06/01/may-30-protests/.
60. Interview with the author, May 2017.

CHAPTER 3
1. Emily Badger and Kevin Quealy, "How Effective Is Your School District? A New Measure Shows Where Students Learn the Most," *New York Times*, December 5, 2017, https://www.nytimes.com/interactive/2017/12/05/upshot /a-better-way-to-compare-public-schools.html.
2. I wrote about Wells Elementary in *HOW It's Being Done: Urgent Lessons from Unexpected Schools* (Cambridge, MA: Harvard Education Press, 2009), and even though I was focused on the school, I was struck then by the cohesive nature of the district.
3. In 2018 the steel mill in Mingo reopened with a promise of hundreds of new jobs. Things were going well until the coronavirus pandemic once again threatened economic disaster.
4. "Steubenville City District Overview," Ohio School Report Cards, Ohio Department of Education, https://reportcard.education.ohio.gov/district /overview/044826.
5. It has since changed the requirement to third grade.
6. There are a lot of good reasons not to have this kind of policy, which is very popular among politicians. Most school districts have not used it as a lever for improvement the way Steubenville has, and I suspect the policy does more harm than good. So I'm not endorsing this policy, just giving the facts.
7. "About CSR," US Department of Education, last modified December 2, 2004, https://www2.ed.gov/programs/compreform/2pager.html.
8. Direct Instruction was developed in the 1960s by Siegfried Engelmann at the University of Illinois and later the University of Oregon and provided curricular material from kindergarten through sixth grade. It is used in very few schools, but has some of the strongest evidence of achievement of any program. There will be more about High Schools that Work later in the chapter. Rebecca Herman et al., *An Educators' Guide to Schoolwide Reform* (Arlington, VA: Educational Research Service, 1999), https://files.eric .ed.gov/fulltext/ED460429.pdf.
9. "Steubenville City District Overview." https://reportcard.education.ohio .gov/district/overview/044826.

10. For an interesting analysis of what happened, see Ariel Levy, "Trial by Twitter," *New Yorker*, August 5, 2013, https://www.newyorker.com/magazine/2013/08/05/trial-by-twitter.

11. Mike DeWine, "Statement As Prepared," Steubenville Special Grand Jury, Steubenville, OH, November 25, 2013, https://www.ohioattorneygeneral.gov/Files/Briefing-Room/News-Releases/Special-Prosecutions/Mike-DeWine-Statement-As-Prepared-Steubenville.aspx.

12. *College Credit Plus: Results and Cost-Effectiveness* (Columbus: Ohio Department of Education and Ohio Department of Higher Education, 2019), http://education.ohio.gov/getattachment/Topics/Ohio-Education-Options/College-Credit-Plus/CCP_Results_Cost-Effectiveness-1.pdf.aspx.

13. The SREB was started after World War II by Southern governors who recognized that the sorry state of their schools was a drag on their economies. Sixteen states are part of SREB. Ohio is not, but it participates in the High Schools that Work program.

14. National Commission on Excellence in Education, *A Nation At Risk: The Imperative for Educational Reform* (Washington, DC: GPO, April 1983), https://www2.ed.gov/pubs/NatAtRisk/risk.html.

CHAPTER 4

1. Since then Reardon has added the smallest districts, including Cottonwood, and according to his analysis of 2016 data, Cottonwood performs 1.25 grade levels above the national average, and students learn 13 percent more every year than the average American student. "Opportunity Explorer," interactive map, Educational Opportunity Project at Stanford University, 2019, https://edopportunity.org/explorer/#/map/ok/districts/avg/ses/pn/10.5/34.28/-95.97/4008730,34.58,-96.17+4017040,34.28,-95.97.

2. By this Reardon meant that third graders were well below the national average, while eighth graders were pretty much at the national average. Emily Badger and Kevin Quealy, "How Effective Is Your School District? A New Measure Shows Where Students Learn the Most," *New York Times*, December 5, 2017, https://www.nytimes.com/interactive/2017/12/05/upshot/a-better-way-to-compare-public-schools.html.

3. Oklahoma hasn't made data journeys easy. It reports a lot of data, but not always in ways that are easy to interpret. And it seems it changes how it reports data every couple of years, which makes it hard to see trends over time. Here is the latest iteration: "Lane, 2018–19," Oklahoma School Report Cards, https://www.oklaschools.com/district/achievement/49/.

4. Current enrollment is closer to 350.

5. Louisa Moats, *Teaching Reading Is Rocket Science: What Expert Teachers of Reading Should Know and Be Able to Do* (Washington, DC: American

Federation of Teachers, June 1999), https://www.aft.org/sites/default/files/reading_rocketscience_2004.pdf.

6. Catherine E. Snow, M. Susan Burns, and Peg Griffin, eds., *Preventing Reading Difficulties in Young Children* (Washington, DC: National Academies Press, 1998), doi: 10.17226/6023; National Reading Panel, *Teaching Children to Read: Reports of the Subgroups* (Washington, DC: National Institute of Child Health and Development, 2000), https://www.nichd.nih.gov/sites/default/files/publications/pubs/nrp/Documents/report.pdf.

7. For one of the many available explanations of whole language, see: Ken Goodman, *What's Whole in Whole Language*, 20th anniversary ed. (Berkeley, CA: RDR Books, 2005), pp. 3–7, https://newlearningonline.com/literacies/chapter-5/goodman-on-whole-language.

8. Daniel Willingham, *The Reading Mind: A Cognitive Approach to Understanding How the Mind Reads* (San Francisco: Jossey-Bass, 2017).

9. At this point there are few people who continue to push pure whole language. Most adherents have long accepted that there needs to be some instruction in sounds and letters; resistance now centers on how explicit and systematic it needs to be. For an extended discussion of reading instruction, I recommend the podcasts of American Public Media's Emily Hanford: "Hard Words: Why Aren't Kids Being Taught to Read," September 2018; "At a Loss for Words: How a Flawed Idea Is Teaching Millions of Kids to Be Poor Readers," August 2019; and "What the Words Say: Many Kids Struggle With Reading—and Children of Color Are Far Less Likely to Get the Help They Need," August 2020; https://www.apmreports.org/collection/documentaries.

10. See, for example, Sally Shaywitz and Bennett Shaywitz, "The Neurobiology of Reading and Dyslexia," *Focus on Basics* 5, issue A (August 2001), http://www.ncsall.net/index.php@id=278.html.

11. In 2007, What Works Clearinghouse reviewed the research and found that Voyager had "potentially positive" effects on alphabetics. The program has been sold to a new publisher and may have changed enough elements that this research may not be fully representative any more. Institute of Education Sciences, *WWC Intervention Report: Voyager Universal Literacy System* (Washington, DC: US Department of Education, August 13, 2007), https://ies.ed.gov/ncee/wwc/Docs/InterventionReports/WWC_Voyager_072307.pdf.

12. The economy of Cottonwood and the surrounding area is very dependent on the price of oil. When oil prices drop, poverty increases; when oil prices rise, a nearby oil field goes into production and poverty drops. The percentage of children qualifying for free and reduced price lunches never drops much under about 60 percent.

13. Not long after she left Cottonwood, Brecheen was named director of early literacy for the state of Oklahoma. She recruited dozens of reading

specialists from all over the state and provided them with up-to-the-minute training from nationally known reading researcher Louisa Moats and other experts in reading instruction. She was trying to undo the fact that many teachers still embraced the whole language philosophy, though it has often been softened to "balanced literacy." Balanced literacy doesn't have an official definition but it usually includes some instruction about sounds and letters while rejecting explicit, systematic instruction. Whole language, Brecheen said, "was the worst thing that ever happened to education." I had enormous hopes that Oklahoma would make a leap in terms of literacy under her leadership, but Brecheen soon found herself ousted by the newly elected Republican state superintendent. She attributed her ouster to her emphasis on looking at realistic data, such as the National Assessment of Educational Progress, that showed a clear picture of how few Oklahoma students read well.

14. Before he left Lane, Smith made a video to try to convince Oklahoma policy makers to support K–8 school districts like Lane and Cottonwood, and it has lots of footage of Lane. Readers who want to hear what parents, teachers, and students say about Lane, can go to https://www.youtube.com /watch?v=Xkun2oaBDNg&t=1s.

CHAPTER 5

1. Memorial service for federal judge Collins Seitz. "Federal Judge Tribute," filmed January 29, 1999, in Wilmington, DE, C-SPAN video, https:// www.c-span.org/video/?119978-1/federal-judge-tribute. When Seitz was a state judge in the 1940s and 50s he ruled twice that Delaware's schools for Black students were not equal to the schools for white students and therefore could not remain separate under the law. His second ruling was appealed by the state and was rolled into three other cases that collectively became known as *Brown v. Board of Education*. While researching Seaford's story I got sidetracked by the fascinating role Delaware has played in school integration, and made it the subject of a podcast: "Segregation, Integration, and the Milford 11," May 17, 2019, *ExtraOrdinary Districts* podcast, https://edtrust.org/extraordinary-districts/special-edition-segregation -integration-and-the-milford-11/.

2. At the rate they were going, they might have closed the gap between Black students in Seaford and white students in Delaware in 2020, except that the state suspended assessments for the coronavirus pandemic.

3. Karin Chenoweth, *It's Being Done: Academic Success in Unexpected Schools* (Cambridge, MA: Harvard Education Press, 2007).

4. Frankford is now John M. Clayton Elementary School.

5. For a discussion of whole language, see the chapter on Cottonwood and Lane, Oklahoma.

6. Reading First got caught up in a question of whether some programs were favored over others because of political connections—a question raised in a lawsuit by Robert Slavin, who objected that the program he had helped create, Success for All, had not been included in the approved list of programs despite considerable evidence that it helped students learn to read. Although several statewide studies found that Reading First helped boost students' reading skills, a big national study found that it did not. I thought that study was flawed and did not prove anything about the effectiveness of Reading First, but the program's reputation was damaged both by the study and the lawsuit, and it ended in 2009.
7. The Blue Ribbon program is a recognition by the US Department of Education.
8. A full list of the Bookworms books can be found at https://openup resources.org/bookworms-k-5-reading-writing-curriculum/.

CHAPTER 6

1. Amy Stuart Wells et al., *Divided We Fall: The Story of Separate but Equal Suburban Schools 60 Years After* Brown v. Board of Education (New York: Center for Understanding Race and Education, Teachers College, May 2, 2014), https://www.tc.columbia.edu/i/a/document/31307_FinalReport.pdf.
2. Ann Choi et al., "Long Island Divided," *Newsday,* November 17, 2019.
3. Josh Anisansel, "Economically Disadvantaged Students Achieving at High Levels: A Case Study," (EdD diss., Fordham University, 2017), https://research.library.fordham.edu/dissertations/AAI10280009/. This is exactly the kind of research that needs to happen, it seems to me.
4. All this data is from the New York State School Report Card found at data.nysed.gov.
5. More formally, these are known as phonemic awareness, phonics, and fluency. I'm oversimplifying what is known as the Science of Reading. For more, read Mark Seidenberg, *Language at the Speed of Sight: How We Read, Why So Many Can't, and What Can Be Done About It* (New York: Basic Books, 2018), and Louisa C. Moats, "Teaching Reading *Is* Rocket Science: What Expert Teachers of Reading Should Know and Be Able to Do," *American Educator* (Summer 2020), https://www.aft.org/ae/summer2020/moats, an update of the groundbreaking work the publication did two decades ago to bring the science of reading to the field of education.
6. Karen Springen, "Fourth-Grade Slump," *Newsweek*, February 18, 2007.
7. Needless to say, the district has horrendous gaps in test scores, which I wrote about in a column for the *Washington Post*. Karin Chenoweth, "As Long as Montgomery County Fails to Teach Children to Read, It Will Have Gaps," *Washington Post*, March 12, 2020.

8. Cognitive scientist Daniel Willingham of the University of Virginia is the person who has provided me with the most background knowledge on reading instruction. See, for example, *The Reading Mind: A Cognitive Approach to Understanding How the Mind Reads* (San Francisco: Jossey-Bass, 2017). Willingham has also made a series of videos, one of which is titled, "Teaching Content Is Teaching Reading," January 9, 2009, https://www .youtube.com/watch?v=RiP-ijdxqEc.
9. I have focused heavily in this book on reading instruction, but all the districts profiled have applied the same general principles that I describe for reading instruction to math instruction.
10. Jack M. Fletcher et al., "Alternative Approaches to the Definition and Identification of Learning Disabilities: Some Questions and Answers," *Annals of Dyslexia* 54, no. 2 (December 2004), pp. 304–31.
11. This is what I call "well, duh" research. That is, research that seems obvious but took a lot of work to establish and counters deeply seated practices.
12. That's the general idea of RTI. Different schools and districts may have somewhat different procedures.
13. Rekha Balu et al, *Evaluation of Response to Intervention Practices for Elementary School Reading*, NCEE 2016-4000 (Washington, DC: National Center for Education Evaluation and Regional Assistance, Institute of Education Sciences, US Department of Education, November 2015), https://files.eric .ed.gov/fulltext/ED560820.pdf.
14. This is what Carol Leveillee found when she arrived at Frederick Douglass Elementary School in Seaford, Delaware, which I described in chapter 5.
15. I will confess that hearing that Journeys was the district ELA program gave me pause. It is a rather standard textbook series that does not score well on Ed Reports, a service that assesses curricula for how well they help students meet standards. I even called reading researcher Jack Fletcher to ask him what he thought of a district that used it. He said he thought there was plenty to like about Journeys, as long as teachers understand how to use it. "What's more important than the program is the professional development," he said. And this is where it is important to note that I didn't talk with a single teacher who said that Journeys was anything more than a resource for teachers. "It's a good place to start," said one. "And then it's what you make of it." This points to the general point that I make in the Conclusion, that programs don't solve problems; they are tools that allow teachers to solve problems.

CONCLUSION
1. Ron Brandt, "On School Improvement: A Conversation with Ronald Edmonds," *Educational Leadership* 40, no. 3 (December 1982), http://www.ascd .org/ASCD/pdf/journals/ed_lead/el_198212_brandt2.pdf.

2. Michael Rutter et al, *Fifteen Thousand Hours: Secondary Schools and Their Effects on Children*, (Cambridge, MA: Harvard University Press, 1982). See Introduction for a longer discussion of Rutter's work.

3. Ronald Edmonds, "Effective Schools for the Urban Poor," *Educational Leadership* 37, no. 1 (October, 1979): 15–24, http://www.ascd.org/ASCD/pdf /journals/ed_lead/el_197910_edmonds.pdf. Actually, Edmonds used the word climate, not culture. I have preferred the term culture since Deb Gustafson, longtime principal of Ware Elementary in Junction City, Kansas, explained how she thought of this question. Climate is a given over which you have no control—you live in an arctic climate or a temperate climate. Culture is how you adapt to and overcome the effects of the climate. I don't think I am altering Edmonds's main point with this change in language.

4. Texas native Molly Bensinger-Lacy, a principal I have written about in previous books, is the person I first heard formulate the issue in that way.

5. For a careful look at the power of variation, see Anthony S. Bryk et al., *Learning to Improve: How America's Schools Can Get Better at Getting Better* (Cambridge, MA: Harvard Education Press, 2015).

6. Three books that are helpful introductions are: National Research Council, *How People Learn: Brain, Mind, Experience, and School* (Washington, DC: National Academies Press, 2000), doi: 10.17226/9853; Daniel Willingham, *Why Don't Students Like School? A Cognitive Scientist Answers Questions About How the Mind Works and What It Means for the Classroom* (San Francisco: Jossey-Bass, 2010); and Benedict Carey, *How We Learn: The Surprising Truth About When, Where, and Why It Happens* (New York: Random House, 2015).

7. See the Introduction for a discussion of them all.

8. This article has links to some of the relevant research: Sanjay Saint, "Hand Washing Stops Infections, So Why Do Health Care Workers Skip It?" The Conversation, May 17, 2016, https://theconversation.com/hand-washing -stops-infections-so-why-do-health-care-workers-skip-it-58763. I wonder if the coronavirus pandemic, in which we were all told endlessly how important it is to wash our hands frequently and thoroughly will improve doctors' handwashing routines.

9. Susan Gates et al., *Principal Pipelines: A Feasible, Affordable, and Effective Way for Districts to Improve Schools* (Santa Monica, CA: Rand Corporation, 2019), https://www.rand.org/pubs/research_reports/RR2666.html. The districts that participated in the Wallace Principal Pipeline Initiative were Charlotte-Mecklenburg, NC; Denver, CO; Gwinnett County, GA; Hillsborough County, FL; New York City, and Prince George's County, MD. Full disclosure: The Wallace Foundation is providing support for this book.

10. I substituted "all people" for the original "all men."

11. As Frederick Douglass put it in his 1850 speech "What to the Slave is the Fourth of July": "Are the great principles of political freedom and of natural justice, embodied in that Declaration of Independence, extended to us?"
12. In the high school my children went to, where three-quarters of the students were students of color and one-third qualified for free and reduced-price meals, parents who started a college fair were told not to bother by teachers and counselors because the students were "just going to be hourly-wage workers."
13. In the Introduction I mentioned *To Sir, With Love*, a movie that depicted a London school in the 1960s. It starred Sidney Poitier as the savior teacher. I can't help but here mention *Blackboard Jungle*, a movie that illustrated the warehousing function of vocational programs in the 1950s, in which Sidney Poitier gained fame as a student angry at his foreshortened opportunities, and Glenn Ford played the savior teacher.
14. I say "all" here. Reading researchers acknowledge that there is a very small number of children whom they have not yet figured out how to teach to read. The children usually have profound cognitive disabilities and constitute 1 or, at most, 2 percent of all children. That doesn't mean they can't learn to read but that the right methods have not yet been formulated.
15. Edmonds, "Effective Schools for the Urban Poor."
16. Robin Steans and Stephanie Banchero, "Chicago Success? Yes," *Chicago Tribune*, October 2, 2015.
17. These are the most prominent of the national acknowledgements of CPS's improvements that I could find: J. Brian Charles, "After Decades of Reform, Has Chicago Finally Learned How to Fix Education?" *Governing*, July 2018, https://www.governing.com/topics/education/gov-chicago-public-schools-education.html; Lauren Camera, "The Secret to Chicago's School Success," *US News and World Report*, April 13, 2018, https://www.usnews.com/news/the-report/articles/2018-04-13/the-secret-to-chicagos-school-improvement; David Leonhardt, "Want to Fix Schools? Go to the Principal's Office," *New York Times*, March 10, 2017, https://www.nytimes.com/2017/03/10/opinion/sunday/want-to-fix-schools-go-to-the-principals-office.html; Kavitha Cardoza, "New Chicago Schools Chief Faces Challenges Despite Strides," *PBS News Hour*, video, April 17, 2018, https://www.pbs.org/newshour/show/new-chicago-schools-chief-faces-challenges-despite-major-strides.
18. I left journalism fifteen years ago to begin working for The Education Trust.
19. In the summer of 2020, Pulitzer Prize–winning journalist Wesley Lowery started a firestorm when he argued that journalists should think less about "objectivity" and more about "moral clarity." I prefer the term political clarity, but am glad Wes Lowery began the conversation.

20. For an interesting discussion of this see Will Bunch, "Saving Journalism's Soul in the Age of Trump," *Noteworthy* (blog), April 19, 2019, https://blog. usejournal.com/saving-journalisms-soul-in-the-age-of-trump-3286d9acc31f.

21. James Anderson, *The Education of Blacks in the South, 1860–1935* (Chapel Hill: University of North Carolina Press, 2010).

Acknowledgments

Educators who are in the thick of running classrooms, schools, and districts are generally too busy to sit down and write their reflections. At some point, I hope all the folks I have written about do share their wisdom—they have a lot to share, and I could only hope to capture a little bit of their experience in this book.

I do want to thank all those who let me in to see what they do and talked with me at length to help me understand the significance of what I was seeing. I can't possibly list everyone, but I want to express my deep appreciation to Janice Jackson, CEO of Chicago Public Schools, whose time and attention is in constant demand but who still found the time to share her insights and wisdom. Thank you also to Mary Beck, principal of Senn High School; Patrick McGill, former principal of Westinghouse High School; Jimmy Lugo, principal of Harriet Beecher Stowe Elementary School; and Cynthia Barron, Paul Zavitkovsky, and Shelby Cosner, all at the Urban Education Leadership Institute at the University of Illinois at Chicago. All helped me better understand school leadership and how it works in Chicago, as well as the teachers who welcomed me into their classrooms, often with no notice. And, of course, Peter Martinez, who was central to so much of CPS's story. Others who helped me understand Chicago's history of improvement are many and include Anthony Bryk, former president of the Carnegie Foundation for the Advancement of Teaching; Elaine Allensworth, director of the UChicago Consortium on School Improvement; Jenny Nagaoka, assistant director of the Consortium; Sarah Duncan, head of the Network for College Success; Terry Mazany, former head of the Chicago Community Trust; Stephanie Banchero of the Joyce Foundation; Heather Anichini, president of the Chicago Public Education Fund; and Jesse Sharkey, president of the Chicago Teachers Union. I owe a special thank you to both Penny Sebring, cofounder of the UChicago Consortium on School Research, and John Q. Easton, senior fellow at the Consortium, for reading early drafts of the Introduction and the chapter on Chicago.

In Oklahoma, I want to thank Pam Matthews, superintendent of Lane Public Schools, and Ashley Willis, principal of Lane Elementary; all the many teachers who took time with me; and, especially, assistant superintendent Sharon Holcomb. She took my phone call out of the blue, invited me to visit, and helped me understand the important work Lane has done over the last decade. I am grateful to John Daniel, superintendent of Cottonwood, who has always been willing to talk frankly about the amazing work that Cottonwood does. The teachers of Cottonwood have been equally generous, which I greatly appreciate. I want to thank both Roland Smith, former superintendent of Lane Public Schools, and Teri Brecheen, former superintendent of Cottonwood, for walking me through the early days of their districts' improvement. And thank you to Anthony Dillard and Todd Hughes of the Choctaw Nation of Oklahoma for providing additional insight into the importance of the work both districts are doing.

In Steubenville, I can't say enough about how much Melinda Young has taught me about school and district improvement through the years, from the time she became a principal to now, when she is superintendent. I find her clear-sighted idealism heartening. I also want to thank former superintendent Richard Ranallo, school board member William Hendricks, principal Teddy Gorman, principal Lynnett Gorman, teachers Natalie Campana, M. J. Burkett, and many more, who took time from their busy days to talk me through the ways Steubenville operates.

In Seaford, Delaware, I want to thank former superintendent David Perrington, who welcomed me into the district, and Corey Miklus, the current superintendent, who not only shared his insights into how the district has improved but also some of the challenges it faces in the age of coronavirus. Principals Becky Neubert, Kirsten Jennette, Carol Leveillee, Laura Schneider, and assistant principal Chandra Phillips, as well as many teachers, all provided insight into what constitutes a functional district that supports improvement. School board member Michael Kraft also shared insights into the kind of advocacy we should be able to expect from all school board members. Sharon Walpole, professor at the University of Delaware, not only provided me with what felt like a graduate-level course on reading jammed into one afternoon but, when that afternoon stretched into the evening, fed and sheltered me so I wouldn't have to drive home late at night. I was honored to speak to Norman Poole about Seaford's history while sitting in the Norman N. Poole Community Center. And, of course, Sharon Brittingham not only pointed me in the direction of Seaford but also helped me understand the larger context of the work being done there.

In Valley Stream 30, not only did superintendent Nicholas Stirling welcome me into his district, he allowed me to share his pride in his students and his joy in providing them with a state-of-the-art learning lab. He makes what he does look almost effortless, the mark of a real expert. Thank you to principals John Singleton, Christopher Colarossi, and Erin Malone; former principal Alejandro Rivera; assistant principals Michael DeBlasio and Yannie Chon; and all the many teachers, parents, and central office administrators I spoke with. And thank you to Josh Anisansel, whose doctoral thesis confirmed early on that I had found a great story in Valley Stream 30.

In writing this book I drew on what I have learned from many other educators through the years. I won't name them—I have acknowledged many of them in previous books—but I just want them to know I continue to try to channel their wisdom.

In some ways this entire book is an acknowledgement of the work of Sean Reardon, Professor of Poverty and Inequality in Education at Stanford University, but I do want to thank him for his help navigating his data. And thanks to his student Heewon Jang for her work on all but one of the charts in this book.

Steve Tozer, professor emeritus at the University of Illinois at Chicago, gets my undying gratitude for his help in thinking through some of the key questions I wanted to answer in this book and his astute critiques of early drafts of some of the chapters. This is a better book because of him.

And I want to thank Nicholas Lemann, who issued a challenge some years ago to education writers to "use both research and the kind of ethnographic work that journalists are trained to do to make sense of the widespread assertions of inferiority or even failure in the American public school system." Those words spurred me to try to answer that challenge, and he was generous enough to read a draft of the introduction and urge me to consider expanding it to a book. My friend Tom Ricks provided similar encouragement at just the right moment.

I am enormously grateful to The Education Trust, which hired me in 2004 to find and learn from schools that help children of color and children living in poverty learn to high levels. They have allowed me to take a long journey through some amazing schools and districts to learn from educators who have a great deal to share with the rest of the profession. It has been an honor to do that work side by side with smart colleagues dedicated to ensuring that all children are served by their public schools. Thank you especially to Ed Trust's president, John B. King, whose smarts, optimism, and generous spirit would buoy anyone's spirits.

I want to thank The Wallace Foundation not only for supporting the writing of this book and some of the reporting that underlies it but for putting the issue of school leadership onto the national policy agenda. The folks at Wallace have worked doggedly to ensure that we have good research about leadership and that the nation can act on that research to build a better principal corps.

Nancy Walser has been a cheerleader, a keen observer, and a nudge. In other words, I couldn't have asked for a better editor, and I feel very lucky to have found a publishing home with the terrific folks at Harvard Education Press.

I feel as if I have to acknowledge the remarkable conditions under which this book was written. I did most of the reporting from 2017 to 2019. Just as I was considering more travel in the spring of 2020, the coronavirus pandemic hit, rendering all reporting trips impossible and forcing me to rely on phone calls and email for all my lingering questions. For all practical purposes, self-isolating from a pandemic and writing a book are the same. But even sitting on the couch with my laptop it became clear that the nation was dealing with multiple crises, of which the pandemic was only one. Once again, we are seeing attacks on universal suffrage, African American bodies, and public schools. These aren't separate phenomena but an assault on democracy waged by those who do not feel a kinship with and respect for fellow citizens but rather seek to separate and dominate. By the time this book is published we should have some answers about whether the nation will continue down the path of autocracy or choose the path that leads toward democracy. Either way, there is a lot of work to be done, and educators have an enormous responsibility for the future of the country and its citizens. I stand in awe of all of the educators who give me a reason to hope, some of whom are in this book.

And, finally, I want to thank David who kept me fed during the writing process—no mean feat in a pandemic—and Emily and Rachel, who are off pursuing their own socially distant lives but still provide me with enormous joy.

About the Author

Karin Chenoweth is the writer-in-residence at The Education Trust, a national education advocacy organization that works to improve the academic achievement of all children, particularly children of color and children who live in poverty.

She is author of four books previously published by Harvard Education Press:

Schools That Succeed: How Educators Marshal the Power of Systems for Improvement (2017);

Getting It Done: Leading Success in Unexpected Schools, coauthored with Christina Theokas (2011);

HOW It's Getting Done: Urgent Lessons from Unexpected Schools (2009); and

It's Being Done: Academic Success in Unexpected Schools (2007).

She is also the creator of the *ExtraOrdinary Districts* podcast and its pandemic spinoff, *ExtraOrdinary Districts in Extraordinary Times.*

A longtime education writer, she wrote a weekly column on schools and education for the *Washington Post* for five years and for several years wrote regular posts for *Huffington Post* and the now-defunct *Britannica Blog.* She was senior writer and editor at *Black Issues In Higher Education* (now *Diverse*); reporter and editorial editor of the now-defunct *Montgomery Journal*; and a stringer with a byline for UPI reporting from Ankara, Turkey. Her work has appeared in *Education Week, Kappan,* and *Educational Leadership*. She graduated from Columbia University's School of Journalism in 1979.

Index